How to
Open & Operate
a Financially
Successful Collection
Agency Business

With Companion CD-ROM

Kristie Lorette & Emonica Dames

HOW TO OPEN & OPERATE A FINANCIALLY SUCCESSFUL COLLECTION AGENCY BUSINESS: WITH COMPANION CD-ROM

Copyright © 2014 Atlantic Publishing Group, Inc.
1405 SW 6th Avenue • Ocala, Florida 34471 • Phone 800-814-1132 • Fax 352-622-1875
Website: www.atlantic-pub.com • Email: sales@atlantic-pub.com
SAN Number: 268-1250

Library of Congress Cataloging-in-Publication Data

Lorette, Kristie, 1975-
How to open & operate a financially successful collection agency business : with companion CD-ROM / by Kristie Lorette and Emonica Dames.
p. cm.
Includes bibliographical references and index.
ISBN-13: 978-1-60138-283-2 (alk. paper)
ISBN-10: 1-60138-283-9 (alk. paper)
1. Collection agencies--United States--Handbooks, manuals, etc. 2. Collecting of accounts--United States--Handbooks, manuals, etc. 3. New business enterprises--United States--Management--Handbooks, manuals, etc. I. Dames, Emonica, 1978- II. Title. III. Title: How to open and operate a financially successful collection agency business.
HG3752.7.U6L67 2012
658.8'8--dc22
2010031315

Printed in the United States

INTERIOR LAYOUT: Antoinette D'Amore • addesign@videotron.ca
COVER DESIGN: Jacqueline Miller • millerjackiej@gmail.com

Printed on Recycled Paper

A few years back we lost our beloved pet dog Bear, who was not only our best and dearest friend but also the "Vice President of Sunshine" here at Atlantic Publishing. He did not receive a salary but worked tirelessly 24 hours a day to please his parents.

Bear was a rescue dog who turned around and showered myself, my wife, Sherri, his grandparents Jean, Bob, and Nancy, and every person and animal he met (well, maybe not rabbits) with friendship and love. He made a lot of people smile every day.

We wanted you to know a portion of the profits of this book will be donated in Bear's memory to local animal shelters, parks, conservation organizations, and other individuals and nonprofit organizations in need of assistance.

– Douglas & Sherri Brown

PS: We have since adopted two more rescue dogs: first Scout, and the following year, Ginger. They were both mixed golden retrievers who needed a home.

Want to help animals and the world? Here are a dozen easy suggestions you and your family can implement today:

- *Adopt and rescue a pet from a local shelter.*
- *Support local and no-kill animal shelters.*
- *Plant a tree to honor someone you love.*
- *Be a developer — put up some birdhouses.*
- *Buy live, potted Christmas trees and replant them.*
- *Make sure you spend time with your animals each day.*
- *Save natural resources by recycling and buying recycled products.*
- *Drink tap water, or filter your own water at home.*
- *Whenever possible, limit your use of or do not use pesticides.*
- *If you eat seafood, make sustainable choices.*
- *Support your local farmers market.*
- *Get outside. Visit a park, volunteer, walk your dog, or ride your bike.*

Five years ago, Atlantic Publishing signed the Green Press Initiative. These guidelines promote environmentally friendly practices, such as using recycled stock and vegetable-based inks, avoiding waste, choosing energy-efficient resources, and promoting a no-pulping policy. We now use 100-percent recycled stock on all our books. The results: in one year, switching to post-consumer recycled stock saved 24 mature trees, 5,000 gallons of water, the equivalent of the total energy used for one home in a year, and the equivalent of the greenhouse gases from one car driven for a year.

Disclaimer

The material in this book is provided for informational purposes and as a general guide to starting a collection agency only. Basic definitions of laws are provided according to the status of the laws at the time of printing; be sure to check for a change or update in laws. This book should not substitute professional and legal counsel for the development of your business.

Table of Contents

How to Open & Operate a Financially Successful Collection Agency

The purpose of this book is to serve as a guide for people interested in learning more about starting and operating a collection agency. This book goes beyond the basics of how to make collection calls, write collection letters, and set up an office. It delves into the everyday responsibilities, issues, and possibilities of having your own collection agency. If you are reading this book, you probably are considering or are in the early stages of starting a collection business. You have made a very wise decision because the collection field can be a lucrative and rewarding career. Whether you have extensive collection experience or none at all, the information in this book will guide you in the right direction to either hone or develop the skills necessary to be a successful agency owner.

This book is designed to answer all the questions you have along the journey of collection-business ownership. The field of collection is complicated enough on its own without having to figure out how to build a business

plan or develop marketing strategies. This comprehensive guide will help you learn what you need to know to be a successful business owner, as well as affording you the opportunity to work within the collection industry.

The collection industry has many laws and regulations. One of the first things you must do is study the laws and be aware of changes and revisions. The two most important laws and regulations are the Federal Debt Collection Practices Act (FDCPA) and the Fair Credit Reporting Act (FCRA). Not knowing these laws could be the death of your new business. Other laws will be discussed in Chapter 11 and throughout this book. Understanding them is crucial to your business' success.

Debt collection agencies serve as the intermediary between a creditor and a debtor. A creditor is the company that originally extended the debt, loan, or credit account to the customer. Depending on the services your agency will offer, the collection agency might take on the responsibility of collecting outstanding debt, reporting to credit bureaus, and possibly submitting the debts to an attorney to sue the debtor. Despite being highly regulated, debt collection is a multibillion-dollar industry, which illustrates how lucrative a collection business can be.

When numerous debtors default on their debt, the creditor suffers multiple losses at once. Most creditors go into business to build relationships and make money because these relationships are essential for company success. However, when creditors do not receive payments or cannot reach customers to work out payment arrangements, creditors are left with no choice but to resolve payment issues aggressively. Once the creditor has done everything they can to try to collect on the debt, creditors look to collection agencies to collect the debt on the creditor's behalf before taking a loss on the debt and writing it off.

The 2008 economic recession has left more people and businesses in debt, which created an environment full of opportunities for collection agencies. As the economy recovers and the unemployed become employed again, debtors have a bigger motive to collect on large debt and loans. Much of the collection process will be done by experienced, reliable agencies.

Debt is everywhere. Most people and businesses accumulate more debt than they are willing to or capable of reimbursing Many have been bamboozled into bad deals, took on more than they can afford to pay, never had any intentions of paying a creditor back in the first place, or have suffered a major financial hardship, such as racking up medical bills from a major illness in the absence of health insurance. Even countries are in debt to one another. One of the wealthiest countries — the United States — has an outstanding debt of more than $14 trillion as of July 2011, with more than $600 billion of this debt owed to Japan. However, the United States is not alone in this problem; nations worldwide are struggling economically; China and India each had their fair share of economic woes in 2008 and 2009.

The History of Debt Collection

The practice of debt collection has been around in its unpolished form since ancient times. Cases date back to biblical times when people purchased items on credit by using their homes, cattle, or even themselves as collateral. When the creditor returned to collect the money, or the collateral, they expected the customer to have the funds to cover the debt. If the customer could not pay as agreed, they could very well have lost their home, cattle, and freedom, as they would have to spend days, weeks, or months working for the creditor to pay off the debt.

Of course, the collection industry changed over the years. Instead of cattle as collateral for property, consumers started putting up other material items — more modern items. By the 1920s, installment plans were introduced for the first time, which permitted consumers to buy items, such as automobiles, directly from the manufacturers and dealers. This, too, changed the collection industry because there were more formal procedures and even collection businesses in place to help keep up with the modern times.

Over time, credit cards evolved, which allowed credit card holders the instant gratification of owning a product or partaking in a service now and paying for it later. The 1930s brought more products and services to the market. During this time, retailers and companies offered their own credit options, such as charge accounts. Again, this provided opportunities for instant gratification but also increased the debt level of the average American.

As the 20th century turned into the 21st century, consumers found themselves in even more debt than they were in during the early 1900s. However, businesses have a more difficult time recovering what is due because of laws, regulations, and guidelines in place to monitor processes, ensure fair completion on debt collection, and protect consumers.

The first third-party collection companies started during the 1920s and 1930s, born from the large amount of credit accounts consumers had opened, but creditors were having a hard time collecting the money. During this time, collection professionals performed a lot of manual labor, such as writing down the details of conversations and account information on paper or note cards. Early collection professionals took collection one step further by visiting debtors at their homes. Today, not much has changed in the tactics used to collect on a debt from a client, except for going door-to-door and manual note- taking. With the emergence of technology, such as the telephone and the Internet, collection professionals have the ability to correspond with debtors from the comfort of an office.

Collection companies put a lot of effort and spend a lot of money to find debtors on behalf of their clients. After locating the debtor, the accounting department spends time proactively working to collect debt.

If a company that has debtors is too small to have a collection department, it is likely the company will hire a third-party collection agency to take care of their collection. Another reason for a company to hire a third-party collection agency to collect debt is experience; collection professionals have the expertise and knowledge of the law to work with debtors amicably, effectively, and efficiently. Furthermore, a business can maintain its reputation by not pursuing the difficult and sometimes unpleasant responsibilities of making people pay what is owed, so it allows the company to remain the "good guy" and the collection agency the "bad guy."

The Current State of Collection

People often view collection companies in a negative light, regardless of their experience. This is because they would rather start paying off their debt at their own discretion. On top of this, in the past, several collection agencies acted as aggressive, non-law-abiding bullies — with a "recover funds, no matter what the cost" attitude. This poor behavior might have included calling the debtor names, threatening bodily harm, and even informing a third party about the debtor's situation. Much of this behavior is the reason the Federal Trade Commission (FTC) has enacted so many laws, such as the Fair Debt Collection Practices Act (FDCPA) to protect consumers from fraudulent dealings by collection agencies.

According to the *Denver Business Journal*, in 2010, the Denver-based collection agency David Faith Corp. was under investigation for allegedly withdrawing money from the bank account of a supposed debtor without his or her knowledge or permission. The FTC keeps these unlawful dealings from occurring.

Fortunately, not all agencies fall under the category of bullies; most are law-abiding, responsible entities. A few tips for standing out as a top-tier, respectable agency include:

- Understand and abide by the laws that govern the industry.
- Treat consumers respectfully.
- Offer reasonable rates and treat clients well.
- Collect! Collect! Collect! Show the client the money.
- Spend the time and money to professionally market your business.

Industry outlook

According to the 2010-11 edition of the Bureau of Labor Statistics Occupational Outlook Handbook (**www.bls.gov**), employment for collectors is expected to grow nearly 19 percent by 2018. This is faster than the average for all other occupations. In 2008, there were 411,000 jobs available to collection professionals. Therefore, the need for new agencies is great, and you have a good chance of succeeding if you take the time to prepare yourself and your agency in advance. The outlook predicts that new jobs will be created in key industries, such as health care and financial services. Using this industry outlook, familiarize yourself with the different types of collection agencies to help you decide which one is the best for you to open and run.

Things to Keep in Mind

In your new role as an agency owner, you will have the opportunity to offer debtors a sound plan to pay off debt that includes:

- Admitting to financial mistakes and finding a way to resolve the problem.

- Obtaining free copies of their credit reports from **www. annualcreditreport.com/cra/index.jsp**, **www.equifax.com/ home/en_us**, or any other reputable credit report website, so they have a big-picture view of their financial situations.

- Come up with a plan for lowering interest rates and making payment and settlement arrangements.

- Communicate with creditors as often as possible.

Before you delve into the journey of opening your own business, be sure you research the federal and state laws that govern the collection industry. *These will be discussed in Chapter 11.* You do not want to find your business in trouble before it has even gotten off the ground. Operating a debt collection agency can be a financially rewarding venture, but be mindful of the mistakes and the roadblocks you may encounter as you get started. It is important to remember as you begin your journey to opening your own successful collection agency that this is simply a guide for you to follow. It is up to you, as the potential owner, to take the initiative and put to use the tips and information you learn throughout this book.

Chapter 1

What is a Collection Agency?

A collection agency is an independent, third party that helps a business with collecting on money owed to them by their customers, individuals, or companies. Collection agencies typically become involved in the collection process when original creditors have exhausted all other means to collect the outstanding debt from their customers. Because the business has to focus on operations, current customers, and making money, it is typically more cost effective to leverage a third-party agency to collect on the debt. Collection agencies also offer other services beyond calling on debtors, such as skip tracing, accounts receivable management, debt purchasing, and credit reporting.

Collection agencies play an important role in the business cycle and the financial health of consumers. Every year, businesses have several millions of dollars of unpaid invoices and statements sitting on their accounts. This affects the results of a company's fiscal projections. When invoices are processed, accounting departments include them in the quarterly projections for profits. When these invoices are not paid in full, this affects bonuses and borrowing bases. A **borrowing base** refers to money a bank lends to a company based on the value of collateral the company has, such as the receivables of the business. Delinquent receivables cannot be included in these figures, which might adversely affect the amount of money a business is able to borrow.

Some companies have a department with its own collection representatives. Most companies, however, find it more efficient and effective to hire a third-party collection agency to collect on the company's outstanding and overdue debts. Collection representatives help consumers by nudging them in the right direction to pay off their outstanding and overdue debt with a well-thought-out plan that includes professional reminders.

Depending on how a collection agency is set up, it may collect on one or more different types of debt, including:

- Loans
- Credit cards
- Utilities
- Medical bills
- Veterinary bills
- Retail accounts
- Services

- Bad checks (NSF)
- Closed bank accounts

A collection agency can recover business-to-business (B2B) or business-to-consumer (B2C) debt. The type of debt, as described in the previous bulleted list, can apply to both B2B and B2C debt recovery because both consumers and businesses have loans, credit cards, utilities, and bank accounts. When working with B2C collection, laws are in place that govern how and when you can communicate with debtors. A new collection agency should research and understand how to abide by these laws before trying to collect on any debt. The Federal Trade Commission (FTC) governs most of these laws, so, you can get to know the laws and stay abreast on the changes in the laws by visiting the FTC website (**www.ftc.gov**).

Although collection agencies do work on the behalf of creditors, the collection agencies do not fully represent the company as they communicate with a debtor. For example, if the XYZ Credit Card Company hires the ABC Collection Agency to collect on its debts, when the ABC Collection Agency contacts the debtor, they will introduce their own company name and say they are calling on behalf of the creditor. It is important to know that a collection agency does not represent itself as being the creditor. The only time that this is not true is when a business hires a collection agency to oversee their accounts receivable or the billing of a customer for items and services they have requested. This process is called accounts receivables outsourcing, which is when the agency handles the functions of current accounts, such as sending invoices, statements, and processing payments.

A collection agency's client — also known as the **creditor** — is called this because they have extended credit or provided a product or service to a customer or debtor. A customer becomes known as a **debtor** when he or she becomes extensively delinquent on an account. Typically, the creditor has deemed the relationship at a point where they cannot, or choose not, to do business with the debtor unless the debtor makes good on the past-due account. It is to the creditor's discretion to pursue business with a debtor once a delinquent account is paid in full.

The client base of a collection agency is varied; companies, both large and small, use collection services. Its services also span different industries. An agency might have clients in such industries as automobile dealerships, banks, insurance providers, retail stores, and mortgage companies, for example. Generally, any company that extends credit can use the services of collection agencies. Therefore, the industry is rare and is one that really targets just about any business to market its services. A new collection agency might decide to work only with small, medium, or large companies, or a specific industry or region. It is entirely up to the agency. Typically, clients choose to call a collection agency for several different reasons, including:

- A customer becomes delinquent and ceases communication with the creditor
- Invoices and statements are being returned
- A customer's phone is disconnected
- A customer begins to complain about service once the account is delinquent
- A customer moves or changes jobs frequently

Keep these reasons in mind as you decide which types of services you might want to offer your clients.

Why Get into the Collection Business?

One of the great things about the collection industry is that you do not have to have years of experience or a specific academic degree to get started. The responsibilities of a collection representative can be acquired with on-the-job training at an established agency, such as the National Asset Management LLC or by taking advantage of training seminars provided by organizations, such as the Association of Credit and Collection Professionals (**www.acainternational.org**). Perhaps the best part of collection agency practice is that the training can be ongoing; you do not have to become a pro at all techniques of collection before opening your agency.

Obviously, when you start your own agency, you will have to learn other aspects of business operations, especially if you do not have staff members. Some of the areas you will be responsible for when running your own agency are invoicing, purchasing, operations management, and eventually staff management. This is true for any type of small business that you operate, be it collection or something else. Throughout this book, you will find many resources available to help make you a great business owner, on top of running a financially successful collection business.

Collection professionals have varied backgrounds, such as real estate, telemarketing, and sales. Regardless of where they came from, most agency owners enjoy working in collection because it is challenging, rewarding, and — most of all — beneficial. According to IBISWorld™, there are more than 8,000 collection agencies operating in the United States, as of 2010. Because companies large and small and government entities use debt collection, the potential to acquire varied clients and make a substantial profit is almost limitless.

What Does a Collection Professional Do All Day?

In terms of the actual debt collection process, a person who collects debt will spend a lot of time on the phone persuading the debtor to pay an invoice or negotiating and enforcing payment plans. This person most likely will initiate collection letters to be sent out as well. The word "initiated" is used to describe the process of sending out collection letters because, depending on the technology available to the agency, a representative might have to draft letters manually, or they might use software that easily integrates the pertinent information of the debtor and debt into a template and automatically sends out the letters. *For more information about collection software, see Chapter 6.*

Collection representatives, the professionals who collect on debts for the collection agency, have a lot of weight on their shoulders because most agencies have quotas they must meet. If you are starting an agency on your own, you still should consider having some type of quota system in place. You have to keep in mind that time is money, so, the faster you can collect the funds due, the more money your agency can make. You also should have your own quota to make sure your company is in line with making the amount of money you need to cover the business expenses and make a profit.

Dealing with people in debt

Working with debtors also means that you are dealing with the usually negative emotions that go hand-in-hand with being in debt. A good collection agency, however, has a plan in place to protect collection representatives from extreme situations. With this plan in place, you easily will be able to identify signs that a debtor is angry or manipulative, and you will learn to recognize those who will flat out deny their debts. Identifying these signs up front allows you to remain in control of the situation, so you will steer it toward a positive resolution.

The angry debtor

Angry debtors are likely to scream, shout, harass, and threaten. While doing so, they avoid answering your inquiries as to why they have not paid their debts or when they are planning on paying them. This type of debtor wants to strike fear inside of you, so you will stop trying to collect on the debt.

When speaking to an angry debtor, you do not want to elevate your voice to the level of the debtor, which can work to further enrage the debtor.

 Furthermore, if while following the lead of the angry debtor you express your own anger and frustration, you really put the debtor in control of the conversation. Acting the same way as the person on the phone could lead you to say something that could get the agency in trouble. A collection representative has to remain calm and be persistent about persuading the angry person to pay off the outstanding debt. *Chapter 13 covers various forms of collection communications, including phone call conversations.*

The manipulative debtor

A manipulative debtor will do just the opposite of the angry person. He or she quietly will try to work on your emotions by crying and discussing all of his or her problems with you. Many times, the manipulative debtor will speak with a very quiet or whiny voice. At this point, you must be strong in not allowing empathy to take over, though it is OK to have it. It is important not to affirm what the debtor is telling you, but instead express your understanding, and ask him or her to come to a solution for paying off the debt.

The debt denier

Debt deniers will flat out deny a debt and act as if they have no recollection of it. However, they never take the legal steps necessary to dispute it. These proper legal steps include sending a written letter of dispute to the collection agency within 30 days of receipt of the collection letter. When this happens, the collection agency then is obligated to research the debt further to ensure they are dealing with the proper person and either cease collection or provide the debtor with proof or details of the original purchase. Debt deniers might think that by verbally denying the debt they are somehow protected by law. In this situation, your main course of action is to offer to send them all of the facts about the debt. And you have to continue to be persistent with your phone calls and letters.

Depending upon the kind of debt you are collecting, two ways to solve the debtor's situation might be to see if they qualify for a repayment plan or to offer some kind of forbearance or deferment plan. These plans enable the debtor to discontinue monthly payments for an allotted amount of time due to financial hardships, illness, disability, or continuing education.

A Special Kind of Collection: Health Care

Health care collection is a $2 trillion industry with more than $100 billion dollars in bad debt. However, due to the nature of the industry, special care must be taken with health care collection.

Due to the cost of health insurance policies, one in six Americans does not have health insurance coverage. However, these men and women have no way of controlling if and for how long they are sick, so medical attention is still sometimes necessary. If someone cannot afford to pay for health insurance, he or she usually cannot afford to pay a hospital bill of $3,000, $30,000, $300,000, or more. Doctors and hospitals must be compensated for their hard work and services, so collection agencies are imperative to the survival of the medical industry.

 Hospitals have the legal responsibility to protect the information or data received about patient's medical issues and identifying factors, such as a patient's Social Security number. Collection agencies must abide by these laws as well. The law is called The Healthcare Insurance Portability and Accountability Act of 1996 (HIPAA). Learning about this law and ensuring all your employees are following it prevents your agency from being sued or forced out of business. It is just good business to protect the privacy and personal data of all clients. For collection representatives, it means they have to be careful that when they are tracking the debtor patient that the representative does not divulge any personal information to a third party, such as a person who might answer the home phone of the debtor.

Beyond maintaining a customer's privacy, hospitals like to maintain excellent customer service standards. Most hospitals will continue to work with their patients, even if they have an outstanding balance. If you decide to work in health care collection, amicable relationships should be your focus as well. It will be beneficial to train and retrain staff throughout the year on best customer service practices for health care collection.

Working in Accounts Receivables Outsourcing

Accounts receivable outsourcing is another way your agency can make money on collecting money. With accounts receivable collection, the debt is not outstanding. The collection agency essentially is serving as the accounts receivable department for a company. In doing this, the agency works under the client's name and does not pursue hard collection tactics. The agency uses the client's letterhead, envelopes, and invoices to manage receivables. The typical services included in this type of recovery are:

- Making phone calls to resolve issues
- Obtaining payment
- Mailing out notices

Accounts receivable outsourcing pricing structures

Before agreeing to take on a client's receivables, you must have a pricing structure in place. For example, it might not be cost effective for you to take on 1,000 accounts of a small business for $800. The contract of services for accounts receivable outsourcing should include a clause that fees will be adjusted to meet any additional services required. The following is a list of sample price structures to give you an idea of where to start your pricing:

- 200 accounts per month / Fee: $500
- 400 accounts per month / Fee: $1,000
- 800 accounts per month / Fee: $2,000

Types of Collection Agencies

After making a decision to open a collection agency, the next step would be to decide what type of collection to pursue. As you learned in the introduction of this chapter, there are two subcategories of collection: business to business (B2B) and business to consumer (B2C). Within these sub-categories are several other types of recovery services to consider.

Some B2B debt includes

- Business loans
- Bank collection — non-sufficient funds (NSF), bad checks, account closed
- Service debt
- Credit card debt/revolving line of credit debt
- Utilities

Some B2C debt includes

- Health care/medical bills
- Student loans
- Bank collection — non-sufficient funds (NSF), bad checks, account closed
- Child support
- Retail debt
- Service debt
- Credit card debt
- Utilities

As a provider, you do not have to stick to just one category of collection, but you might find that one particular area of debt collection is more lucrative than others. If this is the case, you might decide it is more beneficial for the success of the company to stick to these lucrative areas of collection.

Types of Debt

Your new agency will have multiple opportunities to position itself as an expert in one or more particular debt collection areas, such as credit card and health care. Companies around the world are facing aging receivables

— a document showing the amount owed to the company and the amount of time the debt has been unpaid — and look to collection agencies to help them recover the funds. Therefore, it is important that you become acquainted with the types of debt and the laws surrounding them because there might be some differences in rules for collecting each type of debt and the state with which you are doing business. It is in your best interest to research the details with the Federal Trade Commission and the state's governing agency from where you are trying to collect the debt. For example, if the debtor lives in Florida, you have to abide by Florida's state collection laws.

- **Credit Card** — The value is assessed to a credit card based upon the account associated with the card. For instance, a consumer might have a credit card with Bank A with a credit limit of $5,000. And another individual may have a credit card with Bank B with a credit limit of $500. Many factors come into play when a bank sets a credit limit, including past credit history and income. A credit card holder has to pay close attention to his or her available credit as it relates the credit limit. The available credit is the amount of money available to be charged to a credit card.

  Not paying balances monthly might lead to more problems for the credit card holder as he or she owes the balance on the account and interest is accruing. Excessively making this mistake could cause a credit card holder or customer to become the bank's debtor as the amount becomes overwhelming.

- **Student Loans** — Student loans are loans taken out by individuals attending colleges and universities to pay for education costs. These loans typically have lower interest rates and are subsidized by the government.

Blurb from the Higher Education Act

Student loan debt is different from most in that there is no statute of limitations applied, according to the following statute: Section 484A(a) of the Higher Education Act provides that no statute of limitations bars enforcement action to collect Federal student loans, including collection by offset, lawsuit, or enforcement on student loan judgments. 20 U.S.C. § 1091a (a). State law that would otherwise limit these actions is superseded by Federal law and cannot bar collection action. (**www.ed.gov**). The Fair Credit Reporting Act (FCRA), which is under the governance of the Federal Trade Commission (FTC) (**http://www.ftc.gov/bcp/edu/pubs/consumer/credit/cre27.pdf**), dictates the statute of limitations on other types of debt.

- **Payday Loans** — Payday loans are small, short-term, high-rate loans issued by check cashiers and finance companies. People use this type of loan to hold them over until their next payday.

- **Auto Loans** — Banks or dealers issue auto loans for the purchase of a car, truck, or SUV. If the lender breaches the contract and cannot pay the loan, repossession of the vehicle occurs. If a lender sells the repossessed car for less than what was owed on the contract, the borrower can be held liable for the "deficiency."

- **Bank Loans** (Lines of Credit) — A line of credit, which typically is issued by a bank, is a revolving, open-ended loan by which the borrower may use the money up to a certain limit; the borrower must pay the money back and then can borrow the money again.

- **Utility** — Collection agencies will be called on to collect utilities, including phone, electricity, gas, sewerage, and water bills that have become overdue.

- **Apartment Leases** — Different types of funds are to be collected as it pertains to apartment lease debt. When a renter breaches the contract of their lease, is evicted, and has a remainder of rent due, attorney and court fees, and even property damage fees, the property owner might turn to a collection agency to collect the debt.

- **Child Support** — If there is a court order, the collection agency works with the state agency governing child support.

A note about Child Support Collection

Child support collection typically requires interaction with the state agency governing child support cases, if the client has an open case on file. Working against a child support order to collect on debt might have legal ramifications, including prison, performing community service, and monetary fines. *Chapter 11 provides the legal details involved in collecting debts as a business owner or collection representative.*

- **Retail** — Retail debt is debt incurred by an individual that has purchased products from a retail establishment such as Target or Sears˙. Generally, these are credit cards, but store credit cards as opposed to general credit cards issued by a bank.

Summary

As the agency owner, you have many responsibilities that go beyond the practice of debt collection. You wear many hats — hats that are discussed throughout the remainder of this book. Because of all these hats, you must prepare yourself to be an organized multitasker. It is not important that you do everything perfectly from the start, but that you know what it is that you are supposed to be doing and reach out to the proper people and resources to help you along the way.

Chapter 2

What it Takes
to Start an Agency

ebtors tend to view collection professionals as aggressive bullies, but in actuality, most people in the collection industry are hardworking, respectable individuals trying to do their jobs to the best of their abilities. Good collection representatives understand what actions to take to get a debtor to communicate and pay their delinquent bills. It is as much about psychology as the steps it takes to collect the debt.

Questions To Ask Before Opening Your Business

- Do I have the support of my immediate family?
  - o It is important to consider your spouse, as his or her lifestyle will be affected in the early startup stages, especially when the agency might not be making a profit.

- Do I have 12 to 24 months of living expenses set aside?
  - o If you do not currently have a job or plan to quit a full-time job to start the business, plan to have a minimum of 12 to 24 months of living expenses saved. These funds are not to be confused with startup capital for the business. Another option to consider is working part time while starting the business and to stay working until the business is self-sufficient and turning a profit.

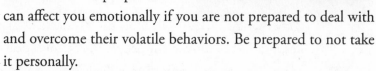

- Am I capable of dealing with the emotional impact of debtors' rudeness and problems?
  - o In this business, you have to deal with toxic people that can affect you emotionally if you are not prepared to deal with and overcome their volatile behaviors. Be prepared to not take it personally.

- Do I have the courage and persistence to look for clients and ask for the sale?
  - o Just because you build it does not mean that they will come. You either will have to have the funds on hand to hire savvy marketing and sales professionals or be willing to network aggressively to find clients and be willing to ask for the sale.

- Am I able to deal with the uncertainty of not knowing when I will be paid?
  - o Regardless of the payment terms set with a client, clients tend to pay on their own schedule, which directly relates to their

own cash flow. This removes the certainty on when and how much you will be paid daily, weekly, or monthly.

- Am I able to rely solely on commission?
  - o The collection business is a commissions-only payment structure, and the commissions might differ based upon the amount or type of debt collected. Again, this payment structure creates uncertainty as to what your daily, weekly, monthly, and even annual income for the business will be. Of course, the money you bring into the business also directly affects your personal income.

- Do I have or can I obtain the startup capital needed to run the business?
  - o If you do not have the expendable capital on hand to start the business, you should have a plan to borrow the money.

- Am I willing to research and abide by the laws that govern the collection industry and protect the rights of consumers?
  - o The collection industry is governed by several laws that must be learned and followed. The Federal Trade Commission enforces most of these laws. You must be willing to follow and keep up with amendments to the laws. Not doing so could lead to the demise of your business.

- Do I have the capabilities or resources to manage all facets of the business?
  - o The facets include marketing, collection, customer acquisition, accounting, and customer service. At first, you may have to manage all of the facets of the business. As the business grows, expands, and prospers, you should be able to hire professionals to handle their area of expertise.

Where am I Going to Open My Business?

There may be zoning restrictions regarding locations where you can start a collection agency. However, each state has registration requirements for starting and maintaining collection agencies in the state.

Zoning for your business

Not knowing where you can operate your collection business can be detrimental to starting the business. Some states have zoning laws in effect for types of businesses, including home-based businesses. Contact the local county zoning office to find out what restrictions are in place for running a home-based collection agency.

You also should contact the secretary of state for the state in which you are opening the business. In the state of Florida, for example, a consumer collection agency needs to register with the Florida Office of Financial Regulation (**www.flofr.com/Finance/Collections.aspx**) and renew the registration annually. At the time of this book's writing, the initial registration fee is $200. The registration period runs year-round. In addition to the registration fee, Florida requires submission of the following information:

- Business or trade name
- Current mailing address
- Principal place of business location
- The full names of each principal registrant or a partner associated with the business
- A statement explaining any occasion on which any professional license or state registration held by the registrant, by any principal of the registrant, or by any business entity (if the registrants were owners of 10 percent or more of the business) was revoked, suspended, or otherwise terminated

Once again, the registration information above is only for the state of Florida. Each state has its own guidelines. Contact your state's financial regulation business office for more information on how to register a collection agency in your state.

The Collection Personality

Every occupation has a personality type or specific traits that are the best fit for individuals working in that profession. This is why human resource directors put such a great emphasis on reading a person or providing testing that gives insight into personalities and characteristics in addition to knowing a job candidate's skills and experience. All positions in the business world require employees to have a hard -work ethic and use tact. In addition to this, a collection professional must be persistent, detail-oriented, assertive, and not easily offended. Persistence is a key characteristic in the industry; if a debtor feels you are not serious about your job, he or she will take advantage of the situation. If you do not exhibit knowledge of all facets

and express complete knowledge of the account and the options for making payments or paying off the account, the debtor recognizes this and might try to take advantage of your lack of knowledge to control the situation.

Skills needed to get the job done

Starting your own agency requires a certain amount of skill, but if you do not currently possess these skills, there is an opportunity to acquire them. One of the primary ways you can garner the knowledge and skills you need is to work as an employee for a collection agency or obtain professional training in the collection industry. Some of the skills you need to successfully operate a collection business include:

- **Negotiation:** You must be able to negotiate with a debtor in order to collect on the debt. Persuading a customer to pay something each time you speak to him or her is a key skill, even if you cannot get him or her to pay the full amount. *Chapter 12 discusses communicating with debtors to negotiate collecting on the debt.*

- **Communication:** You have to be able to communicate effectively to debtors and your clients, in both written and verbal forms. Your client wants to know how you are progressing on the collection and request your advice and suggestions.

- **Investigation:** Investigation skills are necessary because you often have to find out where the debtor lives, works, a new address, and phone number. Other types of legal data also need to be uncovered, including bankruptcies, assets, tax liens, and more.

- **Listening:** You have two ears for a reason; listening is instrumental to your success. Listening intently to a debtor can help you uncover a resource for payment. Further listening to your client can prevent you from having to perform a lot of unnecessary searching and inquires.

CASE STUDY: TRAITS OF A COLLECTION REPRESENTATIVE

Michelle Dunn
President of Never Dunn Publishing LLC
Editorial advisor for Elite
Financial Debt Collection Compliance
Alert Newsletter
michelle@michelledunn.com

Michelle Dunn has more than 20 years of experience working in the collection industry. In 1998, she began her own agency, becoming one of only three women — at the time — to join the American Collectors Association. She recently sold her agency, but because of her personal expertise, Dunn knows the kind of personal traits a collector should possess in order to succeed in the industry.

Dunn says focusing on a win-win situation enables both parties to feel as though they have gotten something out of the state of affairs. "Great bill collectors help their customers or debtors try to solve problems and look for opportunities to make that possible," Dunn says. It is also important that collectors know when to be firm and limit what the representative agrees to to reach a solution that is acceptable for both parties. First, the representative should limit the actions they take to collect the debt because they have to abide by the debt collection laws in place. Second, each consumer is different. A representative that uses empathy with one consumer might have a better chance of collecting the debt than trying to be forceful or pushy, as he or she was with the last consumer.

Patience is another trait that collection agency representatives should have. Dunn says it is easy for many collectors to get caught up in completing the task rather than spending the proper amount of time gathering information so the client feels as though he or she has gotten the their money's worth. "Great bill collectors know that patience is a virtue and that rushing the collection process often leads to not getting paid," she says. Dunn believes that great bill collectors take the time to gather as much information as possible about each debtor because each situation is unique. It is important to collect all of the available information before contacting the customer about the alleged debt.

Along with patience, Dunn says, a successful bill collector needs to be confident and comfortable in the job because of the number of individuals he or she must contact about outstanding debt. "To reach this level of confidence, you must believe in your ability to reach a win-win agreement with the debtor," she says. Dunn attests the confidence she has acquired to the experience she has gained over the years. She says the more debt collection you do, the better representative you will be.

"People will tell you just about everything you need to know," Dunn says. But the key to this is that you need to be confident enough to ask the proper questions or listen long enough to absorb what the debtor is trying to tell you. The biggest mistake you can make as a collector is to interrupt a debtor as he or she explains the situation. Dunn says you miss vital information that could assist you in your collection efforts if you make the mistake of not fully listening.

Resources to obtain the skills to do the job

Many resources are available for you to gain the skills needed to become a successful collection professional. It all depends on your learning style. For instance, if you can soak up knowledge easily by reading books, a trip to your local library or bookstore will be to your advantage. Look for books on negotiation, communication, investigation, and listening. Videos, CDs, and DVDs on these topics are good resources. If reading and watching videos is not the best way for you to learn, consider working part time or temporarily for a collection agency first. Doing this allows you to see when and how to apply the skills by learning from skilled staff members and hands-on training.

If you have the money in your business budget, consider attending collection seminars. Collection seminars cover various topics that range from introducing you to new collection software that is on the market to enhancing and refining your negotiation skills. When you are trying to land clients, any certifications or designations you earn from attending these types of training and educational seminars adds credibility to you and your business, which may ultimately help you to land the client. These seminars vary in pricing and typically are conducted by an association in the industry or independent company that focuses on professional development. A few resources include:

- Collection Training (**www.collectionseminars.com**): This video series training course covers collections topics, such as developing a voice for the telephone, enhancing your listening skills, managing the emotional side of debtors, preparing a pre-call plan, creating the opening statement, asking precise questions, transitioning to the payment arrangement, handling objections, and closing the call.

- Credit and Collections Blog (**www.credit-and-collections.com**): The blog is part of the Credit & Collections Association and is a resource for collections professionals to learn more about the industry and the latest in industry news.

- E-PRG (**www.e-prg.com**): Offers CD-ROM training debt collection and the Fair Debt Collection Practices Act.

Certifications

There are collection associations that offer certifications as well. These are not required but might help to improve your credentials and boost your reputation. If being certified seems to be the way to go, a couple of avenues to start your research are with the National Association of Credit Management (NACM) or the Association of Credit and Collection Professionals

(ACA). After doing your research, if you find a certification that interests you, take a little time to weigh the costs and how it fits into your budget.

According to NACM, the certification program "has helped define and establish professional standards in this demanding and rapidly changing field, and fosters recognition of those individuals who possess special expertise." Certification helps collection professionals pass any exams their state requires for licensing, provides up-to-date information on law and regulation changes, and provides an extra step of credibility to the agency or representative, which can help to win over potential clients. The fee for certification can vary from sponsoring organization to organization, and whether it is for an initial certification or recertification. As of 2011, the NACM charges $225 for members of the organization to become certified and $325 for non-members.

Costs Associated with Starting a Business

You need equipment and supplies to operate your agency. Although you do not need the most expensive supplies and technology available, you should shoot for a balance between cost and quality. Do not make the age-old mistake that many entrepreneurs make — spending exorbitant fees on brand-new, top-of-the-line technology using credit or borrowed money. If the business fails, you are left paying off this debt. Below is a list of technology and supply must-haves for collection agencies:

Technology		Service		Supplies	
Computer	$600	Web hosting $180 (year)		Business cards	$80
Telephone	$50	Web domain — free with hosting*		Letterhead	$130
Copy/fax/scanner	$129	Telephone service $100		Portfolio folders	$16
Accounting software	$300	P.O. Box $80		Basic office supplies	$120
Collection software	$900				
USB backup drive	$30			Brochures	$500
Paper shredder	$120			Fliers	$60
Filing cabinet	$215				
Desk	$150	**Total**		**$3,760**	

Some web-hosting companies will provide you with a free domain name. Most domain names are inexpensive and run in the $10 or so range.

The prices above can change and might be less or more expensive, depending on how much you shop and compare. You might not think you can afford collection software in the beginning stages of your business because prices for this type of software can be astronomical. However, this might be something you should consider spending a little extra money on right at the beginning. This software allows you to organize the collection business, so when it grows, you already have your processes in place. It helps to avoid scrambling to put the software in place when your business has already grown to a point where you cannot control the process or manage it effectively.

Licenses

Licensing guarantees that the service provider has been trained in the proper regulations and procedures of the services they offer. A licensed agency is capable of handling clients in a professional manner. Collection is an industry that requires licensing in most states. It is important to do as much research as possible to learn about the types of licensing for your particular state. In general, the goal of licensing for collection is to ensure your company has taken the time to learn the laws that govern the industry and will execute its duties in a professional manner. Links to websites of all 50 states and U.S. territories can be found at **www.usa.gov/Agencies/State_and_Territories.shtml**. Because each state has its own unique home page design, it might be easier to find information for licensing on some sites rather than others. If you are having a hard time locating the proper page for business licensing, search "business licensing" or "collection agency licensing" on the Web, and you will be given the appropriate links.

For example, to obtain a collection agency license in Florida, you must obtain a licensing application, specifically for a collection agency, from the Florida Department of Financial Services (**www.flofr.com/finance/forms/ccainstruct.pdf**). As of 2011, Florida requires you to submit a completed application and pay a $200 fee.

In the state of New York, a collection agency license also requires an application. Along with the application, you have to provide proof that you have registered the business with the state and what type of entity you have registered it as (corporation, LLC, partnership, etc.). New York also requires proof of a surety bond of $5,000 and some additional debt collection forms signed and submitted with the application. A surety bond is a promise for hired party to pay the hiring party in a transaction if the hired fails to fulfill its obligation. The fee for the license depends on what time of year you file for the license. For example, if you file the application from February 1 in an odd year to July 31 in an odd year, the fee is $150. From February 1 in an even year to July 31 in an even year, the fee is only $75.

Insurance

Licensing and bonding requirements vary from state to state. What you pay for insurance depends on the type of insurance and the coverage amount you choose. Contact a business insurance agent to discuss the specific type of business insurance you need and the amount of coverage you need to get an estimate of cost. To check on the licensing and insurance requirements for your state, visit the official business link to the U.S. Government website at **www.sba.gov**.

Types of insurance to consider for the collection industry

- **Errors and omissions:** Provides protection for collection agencies from lawsuits that stem from normal business practices

- **Crime:** Helps companies protect themselves against internal theft

- **Employment practices:** Protection against employee lawsuits stemming from harassment and wrongful termination suits

- **Cyber liability:** Protects companies in the event that data is stolen via hacking or computer theft

Bonding

Bonding protects a client in the event that a vendor (you) does not fulfill the obligations of a contract. An agency that is **bonded** has employed a bonding company to handle funds that the state oversees in case a client files a claim against the agency. A third party assumes the financial responsibility of the broken contract. Bonding essentially protects the client from gross negligence by the collection agent or if the agency is "stealing" from their client. It returns the client to the position they were before the wrongdoing of the collection agency. Depending on the income potential a particular client might afford you, it might be in your best interest to be bonded because it allows you to land bigger clients who either provide you with a higher volume of accounts or individual accounts with higher collection amounts. However, a bond is not an insurance policy, and there are several types. Bonding might not be required in your state. Check with your planning or zoning department to determine if bonding is a necessity or an option. Even if your state does not require bonding, your clients might want you to be bonded.

Summary

If you are planning to start and operate your own agency, it is necessary to know what constitutes a good representative and CEO — as most likely you will be wearing both hats for a while. Even if you have worked in the collection industry for a while and have a decent recovery record, you should perform a self-evaluation to determine if you are capable and ready to open and operate a successful collection business.

Chapter 3

Deciding How to Set Up Your Agency

N ow that you know the facts of what kind of person it takes to start a collection agency, the next step is deciding where you want to run your business — from a home-based office or a commercial space. Both types of work environments come with their own set of pros and cons. So, you will need to weigh the advantages and disadvantages of each to determine which is the best setup for your business.

Home-Based Business

Working from home has its advantages. You do not have to worry about the additional efforts and fees associated with setting up your offices. For tax and work purposes, it is essential that you have a designated space for your office and running your business. Typically, guest bedrooms, finished attics, or basement areas all make perfect options for transforming into your business office. Because you will be on the phone with both your clients and the debtors, you also should consider setting up your office in a room that has a door, so you can close off your office from any noises and distractions that are in the rest of your home — pets, children, spouses, the doorbell, etc.

Advantages of working from home

Running a business from home definitely has its cost advantages. You can keep your overhead costs to the bare minimum. Some of the other advantages that come with running a home-based business include:

- **Being Your Own Boss:** You are not only the boss of your business, but you also are the boss of your office. You do not have to worry about landlords, other office tenants, and building rules, such as those that come with renting a commercial space.

- **Financial Freedom:** It will be hard at first to make a profit, but a collection business has the potential to make a handsome income. The limitations are based solely on how hard you are willing to work. Working at home allows you to limit your business expenses, such as saving money on extra rent or additional electricity and water bills.

- **Increased Availability to Family:** If you are a parent and prefer being home when your children come home, a home-based business offers you this flexibility. In order for your work life not to suffer, however, it is advisable to set a schedule and stick to the schedule as much as possible.

- **Personal Time:** If you need time off or would like to take a break during the day, you can. You have the liberty to set your own work hours and set your own standards.

- **Tax Benefits:** A home office also provides several types of tax deductions. You typically can write off the rent or mortgage, utilities, insurance, estate taxes, and some repairs proportionate to the amount of square feet your office takes up in your home.

Disadvantages of working from home

The obvious disadvantage of working from home is the likelihood of getting distracted by normal home-life activities. Before getting too excited about starting your new collection business at home, consider all the disadvantages, which might end up outweighing the advantages. The most important thing to keep in mind when deciding between the two office setups is to create a professional business environment that also fits into your budgetary and financial constraints. A few disadvantages of working from home include:

- **Meetings:** If you have a need for face-to-face meetings with your clients, you really do not want to invite them into your home. This means you either have to meet at the client's location or arrange a mutually convenient meeting place.

- **Personal Distractions or Interruptions:** The line of distinction easily can be blurred between your professional and personal time. If you are regimented and motivated enough to separate this time, it may not be an issue. If personal calls, the laundry, your kids, and your dog easily distract you, you might have a hard time working when you should be.

- **Decreased Personal Development/Solitude:** Working at home typically means you are working alone, so your only interaction during your work hours is by telephone. If you need personal interaction with coworkers for stimulation, for professional development, or to stay sane, working alone out of a home office might not be the best setup for you.

- **Lack of Professional Front:** If your kids are crying and your dog is barking while you are on the phone with a client or a debtor, it does not present a professional work environment. If you spend all day working in your pajamas rather than getting dressed and ready for your day, this unprofessional attitude can come through in your conversations with people on the phone. It is important to act and present your business in the most professional manner — always.

Setting up a home office

If you have made the decision that working from home is the right choice for you, it is time to start setting up your office. Try to establish an office space as soon as possible, even when you are still working through the set-up stage of your business because it provides you with the equipment and area you need to conduct research, fill out applications, and get all of the legalities of starting the business in order. Getting your office set up early plays a part in how successful everything is that comes after. If you have to go through construction on your home to turn a space into an office or to create the working environment you need, set up a temporary office so you can find a local, experienced, and licensed contractor to oversee the project. Once you have the space chosen, it is time to fill it with the computer, telephone, file cabinets, desk, chair, and other office supplies you need to start and run the business.

Phone service

Although you can start a business with no more than the above essentials, you probably be more successful if you incorporate a few extras. If you want to be listed in the yellow pages, you will need to have a phone dedicated just to business. Some people use only a cell phone, but a dedicated line is preferable. Although it is more expensive, having a "business only" landline allows you to separate your business calls from your personal calls, establish a business voice mail, and even provide a line to use as a fax line, if you choose. You also will need a fax machine or an all-in-one printer, scanner, copier, and fax machine that can accommodate all of your business needs. You might choose to have a dedicated fax line, or you might choose to use your business line for talk and faxes.

You also should invest in a two-line business phone and make sure your phone service has call waiting. Some phone companies offer a "distinctive ring" feature that rings differently if a fax is coming in, so you do not make the mistake of picking up the phone as if it is a voice call.

Telephone prices vary according to quality and features. Find the best one you can afford. Service providers, such as AT&T™ (**www.att.com**), Verizon (**www.verizon.com**), and RingCentral (**www.ringcentral.com**), are options for setting up a phone line for your new business. These companies allow business phone models with caller ID, auto-receptionist, and automatic dialing. Although you can use a phone with an answering machine built in or add the answering device to a phone, it is typically better to opt for a phone service that provides voice mail. This way, if you are on the other line and cannot or do not switch over to answer the other call, the caller will receive the outgoing message for your business and be able to leave a message. With an answering machine, the phone continues to ring, which might make the caller think they have the wrong number. If he or she hangs up, he or she might not call back, and that could be a lost business opportunity for you. Because you will be spending so much time working on the phone, you also might want to invest in a headset.

Home-based business insurance

Business insurance is another cost you need to consider for establishing and operating your business. Business insurance relates to your business whether it is a home-based business or an off-site business. The amount of coverage you need to carry, and the types of business insurance you carry will vary according to whether you choose to run your business from home or a commercial space. You should speak with the insurance company that carries your homeowner's insurance policy or to your insurance agent to discuss the insurance options you must carry and those that you should consider carrying. Some of the types of insurance you should be aware of include:

- **Business property insurance** — This type of insurance covers the loss of or damage to your business property, including the property structure, the businesses personal property (tables, chairs, and office equipment), damages from flood and earthquakes, and loss of income.

- **Health insurance** — Having this insurance will set you apart from new businesses because many up-and-coming agencies will not be able to offer their employees medical coverage. This should be the very first type of insurance you, as the business owner, look into and research for your own needs, and then extend this as a benefit to employees you hire to work for you.

- **Life insurance** — Although this is not solely for your business, it is important to have. If you should die prematurely, your family will be liable for the bills and expenses of the business you have left behind. Some lenders require you to have life insurance before taking out a loan with them for business startup or operating expenses.

- **Workers compensation insurance** — This is very important if you plan to employ workers. Without this insurance, you will be fully responsible for covering any medical expenses an employee incurs from injuries sustained while performing their normal work duties or because of unsafe work conditions.

- **Business interruption insurance** — Business interruption insurance covers you for time you are not able to operate. Typically, business interruption insurance covers the loss when you cannot operate your business because of a natural disaster or other unforeseen circumstances that affect your business operation.

Home-based insurance is a requirement for running a home-based business because homeowner's insurance policies rarely cover business losses. You should contact your insurance agent, however, to verify what your homeowner's insurance policy covers as far as your home-based business is concerned because the typical policy specifically excludes home-based business losses, including equipment, theft, loss of data, and personal injury. Unfortunately, many companies that provide homeowner's insurance do not offer business coverage, so you might need two insurance companies covering different areas of your home — one for personal use and the other for the business use of the property.

Traditional Office Building

When selecting a traditional office building to start and operate your collection agency, there are factors to consider. Even though you might not have many walk-in customers, you should choose a location that is easily accessible and within a business community. You might want to choose a location near the types of businesses that are your potential clients. For example, if you opt to specialize in medical collection, you might choose a business building near a major medical center, hospital, and doctors' offices in the area. Once you have selected a few viable locations, look closely at the upkeep of the building, and conduct some background research on the property management company. Talking to current renters and walking through the building can prevent moving into a building that has mold, HVAC, or pest problems. Moving into a building that has maintenance issues or tenant discrepancies can cause problems that affect your performance or turn away clients. Look for multiple or pending lawsuits from past and current renters to see if the building is in violation of any codes or ordinances and that the property management company takes care of property issues within a reasonable amount of time.

Working from an office or professional environment helps keep unnecessary distractions away. In addition, it provides you with a professional setting in which you can meet with clients and even network with other professionals. An office space provides you with the room you need to grow and expand your business, such as hiring employees.

The primary disadvantage of renting an office space is the expense. On top of the rent you have to pay on a monthly basis, you typically have the added expense of furnishing and equipping the office with everything you need. In addition to your standard desk and office equipment, you also need to purchase furniture, blinds, and décor to make your working space comfortable and workable.

Another disadvantage is the commute. Depending on where you find the office space to rent, you might have a short or long commute from your home. Because you should try to rent an office space in area that exposes your collection business to potential clients, this might require you to rent space in the downtown area of your city when you live across town in the suburbs, for example.

A third disadvantage is finding the right space for your collection business. It might be difficult to find an office space that fits your size requirements. The setup of the office may be another factor. Perhaps you need a small office separate from the lobby but cannot find something suitable, so instead you have to rent a one-room space and partition it off so you have space for a receptionist and a waiting room.

Running the business out of your home or renting an office space are not the only two options you have for starting and operating your business. Some options fall between these two options. One of these options is collaborative workspaces.

Collaborative Workspaces for the Self-Employed

If you feel the disadvantages of working from home are a viable reason for having an office out of your home but cannot or do not want to face the challenges of leasing an office suite, the next best option is renting space from a collaborative office building. These buildings offer per diem office spaces for individual contractors, so you pay only for the portion of the space you take up in the building, which tends to be much less expensive than renting an entire office suite on your own.

Another advantage of collaborative workspaces is that you use them as you need them. For instance, if you only need to use an office or meeting room to meet with clients, you can pay for the use of the conference room for the entire day or by the hour. If you want to rent a cubicle or office on a consistent basis, you can pay a monthly rate, which again is much less expensive than renting and operating an entire office space alone. Some collaborative workspace buildings charge a nominal monthly membership fee. Beyond the amenities that collaborative workspaces offer, using these offices puts you in a situation to meet and network with other professionals. Many times, the renters help each other by brainstorming and bouncing ideas off each other. This is great because you can get an objective perspective from someone who is not necessarily in the collection industry. To get more of an idea about how these companies work, look at the website of a popular collaborative workspace in Orlando: **www.orlando.colabusa.com**.

Other amenities of collaborative workspaces include:

- Conference rooms
- Office space or room
- High-speed Internet access
- Printers, copiers, fax machines, and other business equipment
- Receptionist
- Mail delivery service
- Depending on the company, there may be other amenities

Basic Office Supplies for any Office Setting

A traditional office and a home office tend to need the same types of office supplies. Because office supplies include everything from paper, pens, and paperclips to fax and copier machines, costs are comparable, unless you opt for a commercial version of the supplies (i.e., a commercial or business copier as compared to an all-in-one copier, scanner, fax, and printer.). In collaborative workspaces, some of the supplies and machines are included in your agreement. Small office supplies, such as paperclips and pens, might not be included, so, you might have to supply these smaller items on your own. Again, it all depends on the agreement you have with the superintendent of the building.

Fax machine, copier, and scanner

Unless you plan to use your local copy store for faxes, you need a fax machine. All-in-one machines are used by many small businesses for faxing, copying, and scanning. The prices are reasonable, and they work well to meet all your needs. The more expensive models have extra features and are more durable. These options are ink-jet printers, not laser machines, which cost significantly more money.

Technology also has improved the ways in which we can fax documents. Online faxing services allow you to fax documents directly from your computer. This service is feasible and provides you with a phone number and

software for transmitting faxes and even receiving faxes, all within your computer. Use the following list of the most popular e-faxing resources to determine which one, if any, is best for your office:

- **www.electronicfax.org**
- **www.efax.com**
- **www.metrofax.com**
- **www.trustfax.com**

Calculator

The collection business is a numbers business, so one of the primary tools you need is a calculator. Invest in a desktop calculator that remains on your desk as a permanent fixture. You might want to opt for an adding machine, or a calculator that prints out receipts of your calculations. You can attach the printouts to the client and debtor files or check your work for accuracy. If you add a zero or two in your calculations, it is easy to identify what the problem is in your calculation so you can easily correct it. When you visit client locations, you should have a portable calculator.

Postage meter

Collection agencies send out many collection letters and other notices, so it might be more convenient to invest in a postage meter. If you are just going to be sending out a few pieces of mail every month to pay bills or send letters, you might not need one. If you work with clients that have the email addresses of debtors, you might use email over regular mail. But if you are going to be sending out mass mailings to potential clients as part of your marketing, a postage machine would be a wise choice. Having a scale and meter combination machine can even prevent you from overpaying for postage, which can occur when you guess the weight and postage for certain mailings, as well as save you a trip to the post office.

Another option to consider is purchasing postage online. Depending on the size of the mail you typically send, this is a good option for collection businesses. It is rare that you will have to send parcels as part of your daily work, and if you need to, you always can use FedEx or UPS. One of the best resources for online postage is the U.S. Postal Service website, **www. USPS.com**. From this site, you can download postage as needed. These services can also be found at **www.stamps.com**. Stamps.com works in conjunction with the USPS. Both services allow you to print stamps directly to your personal printer.

Merchant processing and point-of-sale equipment

Merchant-processing machines, also known as point-of-sale (POS) equipment, allow you to process credit card payments. You may accept credit card payments from clients that hire you to collect on the debt or even from the debtors themselves. Privacy becomes an issue when accepting credit card payments, and you should include a clause in your client agreements or on invoices that spells out your policy for protecting a debtor's personal information. In many states, it is against the law to keep a consumer's credit card information on file for any reason. Each time a payment is processed, you are required to ask for the credit card information.

Merchant-processing equipment and services are becoming more convenient with accessibility to the Internet, terminals, wireless processing, phone processing, and QuickBooks™ processing, which is a software program that allows businesses to run accounting procedures. *Chapter 6 covers more on the capabilities of QuickBooks for small businesses.* It is faster and easier to collect a debt from a debtor by creating a sense of urgency. One way to do this is to tell the person that he or she can pay off the debt right now with you using his or her credit card, which means you need to have a point of sale or credit card processing machine on hand. Credit card processors do not require you to have possession of the credit card, so all you need is the credit card number, name as it appears on the card, billing address for the card, credit card number, expiration date, and the three- or four-digit code on the card. This alleviates waiting to receive checks or money orders from debtors in the mail.

Merchant-account providers tend to find new business owners, so you are likely to receive multiple offers in the mail as you start the process of opening your business. Shop and compare merchant account providers as you would any major purchase. Your first stop should be at your bank. It can be more convenient to have your merchant account with the same bank that holds your business bank account or even your personal bank account. The merchant account is where the money goes when you process credit card transactions. The merchant account is not your business bank account; the merchant account is simply a holding account. You can connect the merchant account with your business bank account so you can transfer the money from the merchant account to your bank account to access the money. You would then pass the money over to your client minus your fees for collecting the debt. Some clients may allow you to use their credit-card processing system, so they receive the money directly from the client and then cut you a check for your fees. If you decide to use your own credit card processor and merchant account, then you, of course, have to weigh the costs and fees associated with the merchant account because banks tend to charge higher fees for these accounts than other types of merchant account providers. Some of the merchant account providers you should check into include:

- **PayPal™ (www.paypal.com)**: PayPal is an online payment service that allows businesses and individuals to accept electronic checks (e-checks) and credit card payments online. PayPal allows the PayPal account holder to connect one or more bank accounts to the PayPal account to transfer the PayPal balance into the business bank account.

- **Merchant Express (www.merchantexpress.com)**: Merchant Express allows businesses to process credit card payments.

Depending on the type of processing you choose, you can process credit card payments online, via phone, by wireless device, or using a credit card terminal machine.

- **Blue Pay** (**www.bluepay.com**): Blue Pay is another credit card processing company that offers myriad resources for processing credit card payments and transferring the money in the business bank account. Blue Pay offers integration with some accounting software programs to simplify your credit card and accounting processes.

- **First Data**™ (**www.firstdata.com**): First Data provides businesses everything from terminal and online credit card processing options to processing credit card payments by phone. First Data also offers mobile credit card processing options.

> **Note:** Most of the time, a debtor prefers not to deal with you face-to-face, so include an online option for them to process credit card and e-check payments on their own. This is an option you need to think about when it comes time to build your business website.

Make sure debtor accounts are updated immediately after all payments are processed. If, for any reason, a payment is later denied, you always can reverse the transaction and immediately contact the person to reprocess the payment.

Additional office supplies

Office supplies are necessary in any business. The minimal office supplies needed are writing instruments, photocopy and printing paper, paper clips, envelopes, ink cartridges, and notepads or notebooks for taking notes. Other supplies include letterhead and business cards. You can purchase office supplies from online providers or from local office supply stores. To cut back on the cost for office supplies, you can opt to buy the generic brand or store brand over the name-brand products. Work quality for office supplies tend to be the same whether you pay 45 cents for the item or $2 for the item.

You might want to consider buying in bulk. Buying office supplies in bulk can save you money and ensures you do not run out of office supplies on a regular basis.

Ink cartridges

Ink can drain your wallet if you do not pay attention to how much is spent on it. The average new ink cartridge costs about $30. If you buy black and color ink cartridges, you can expect to spend around $60. Once again, consider the amount of ink you use. If you do not need to print something, do not print it. If you do not need a color printout of the item, opt to print a black-and-white copy only. There are other ways to limit how much you spend on ink cartridges, including refilling your old cartridges and recycling them. Some suppliers will pay for or offer store credit for recycled cartridges.

Letterhead and business cards

Letterhead and business cards play dual roles; they are office supplies and your business brand or identity. These promotional items and necessary business supplies can promote and represent your company, even when you are removed from the equation, which is why it is critical to have these items professionally printed and available as soon as possible. If you decide to design and print your own letterhead and business cards, especially at first to cut down costs, make sure you print at the highest quality. You might even want to elicit some opinions from people you know on what they think of the cards and letterhead you have designed and printed before you start using them. When you weigh the time it takes to print your own items, plus the cost of paper, card stock, and ink, you might find it is more convenient and cost-effective to have them printed professionally.

Most major office supply stores have people who can help you design high-quality letterhead and business cards.

You also can turn to online printers such as Vistaprint (**www.vistaprint. com**) and 48HourPrint.com (**www.48hourprint.com**). These companies provide quick turnaround times and low-cost options that do not require you to sacrifice quality.

Purchasing a computer for your home, traditional, or collaborative workspace

A computer plays an integral role in your business. Computers aid collection agencies in collecting, storing, and managing large amounts of data, such as client information, payment information, and debtor contact information. Because computers come with all types of features and applications, it can make your choice confusing and difficult. The key is to understand exactly what you need your computer and its software to do---don't

allow the extraneous information to distract you. The next few sections of this chapter help you identify the features and applications you need and which ones might be optional or unnecessary.

Desktop or laptop?

One of the first options is to choose between a laptop and a desktop computer. Both options have benefits and drawbacks. A desktop computer probably tends to have bigger monitors/screens and an easy-to-use keyboard. However, a desktop computer is also not portable like a laptop computer is. A laptop is portable and easy to use, but it also tends to cost more than a desktop. The cheapest route is to select the most powerful desktop you can afford that provides you the most computing power for your money. When you need a laptop, you can purchase one once your business starts to grow, and you have more cash to spend.

Whether you choose to buy a desktop or a laptop, you might want to purchase an external hard drive to back up or archive your document files and other essential records at least once a week to avoid data catastrophes. Back up or copy all important data, such as client and debtor files, invoices, and your financial records at least daily or every time you work on a file.

You also might want to consider an online backup system in addition to backing up your computer locally to an external hard drive. Two reasonably priced options are offered by **http://mozy.com** and **www.ibackup. com**. Regular backups protect your data from electrical blackouts, viruses, and other calamities.

Basic Computer Features Needed

Your computer's speed is an important factor in making the right choice. Although you do not need a lightning-fast computer, which tends to cost more money, you do need a reliable computer. As the business grows and the number of accounts you have increases, you can always upgrade your computer to a better option. Below are some of the basic features to consider when buying a computer.

- 2.5 GHz and above
  - o Processors define the speed at which your computer operates. OEM will use processors from different companies; your goal is to focus on the speed.

- 2 GB to 3 GB of memory
  - o This is enough memory to handle typical memory-hungry applications.

- 250 GB to 320 GB 5,400 hard drive
  - o This is enough space to hold large documents, photos, and videos.

- Wired Ethernet; wireless Wi-Fi
  - o This will allow you to connect to broadband modems. If you will use laptops as well, this provides wireless connection.

- 18" to 22" monitor display (1,680 x 1,050 resolution)
  - o This screen is large enough and clear enough to allow you to easily see and find what you need on the screen without having to squint or continually adjust font size.

Features you may want

- Webcam
  - o This feature is great for virtual meetings.

- 4-in-1 digital media reader
  - o With this feature you will be able to watch videos and listen to music.

You can find a reasonably priced computer with the features above within the price range of $450 to $600. If your budget allows for more, you can increase the size of the basic features, amount of wanted features, or the number of computers you buy for the business.

Basic software

Chapter 6 will discuss the software you need for your business accounting and specifically for the collection aspect of your business. However, here is a brief overview of some of the basic software programs you should have. First, you should load a word-processing and spreadsheet program on to your computer. The most popular software package is Microsoft® Office, which includes Microsoft Word, Excel®, PowerPoint®, and Internet Explorer®. Other software packages exist and are less expensive. If you are using an Apple computer, your operating system will be Mac OS. This might cause compatibility issues if you are creating documents on a PC and then sending them to Mac users, who might have problems opening the documents you send. However, keep in mind that the majority of businesses use Microsoft. You do not want to be in a position in which you are not able to receive or transmit documents to a client because you are not in sync with the rest of the business world.

Adobe offers many products, but the one typically used is Acrobat® Reader; it allows you to make PDF files.

Internet service providers

The Internet typically plays an integral part of a collection business because it gives you access to the resources you need to track down debtors, conduct research, email information to clients and debtors, and even promote and market your business. Hence, Internet access is necessary for your business, whether your office is at home, in a collaborative workspace, or in a rented office. Fortunately, you have options, including Ethernet and Wi-Fi features for wireless connection. High-speed Internet and DSL access provide you with faster Internet service. Because time is of the essence in a collection business, having and using as fast an Internet connection that fits in your budget is a necessity. Most telephone and cable service companies offer Internet services. The monthly expense for Internet access generally runs between $20 and $40 per month. You also can get a package or bundled deal if you obtain phone, cable, and Internet services with the same provider.

Computer security

Firewalls and virus protection programs are essential tools in computer protection, no matter what type of business you are in, so you need them for your collection business as well. European Union computer security experts estimate that in 2007, viruses began to attack new computers on the Internet within seconds. Firewalls, whether hardware, software, or a combination of the two, protect your computer from unwelcome intrusions by outsiders and unauthorized individuals.

Antivirus software protects your computer from viruses and is software that must be purchased. Different levels of protection are offered, so prices will vary depending on how much protection you will want and need. Symantec™, McAfee®, and Norton™ are among the best-known software providers of this type of protection. Their programs must be updated regularly — preferably every day — to guard against the latest viruses, so you will want a renewable subscription that is usually less than $100 annually for the basic protection. If you have multiple computers, you can opt for packages that cover a set number of computers.

If you are already familiar with computers, you are probably conscious of spammers who send out millions of email messages for unwanted products or services, and the phishing schemes that come along with this email to try to obtain your personal information. If not, dishonest computer hackers constantly try to steal your passwords, bank account numbers, and other personal or business identity information to steal your money or your identity. The simplest way to protect yourself is to never click a link sent by someone you do not know, especially if the person claims to be a "webmaster" at a bank, your Internet service provider, or some other legitimate-sounding source. If you are doubtful, call the company that is supposedly requesting the information from you. You want to make sure you have every resource available to help protect your computer against the latest schemes of hackers who want to access your bank accounts, credit cards, passwords, and all of the other information you need to protect.

Summary

It might seem overwhelming to consider all of the needs you require for your business. Needs range from the technology and office equipment required to run your business to determining the kind of employees that would be a best fit. But the most important thing to remember when considering something for your agency is always to invest in the items or people that will enhance — not hinder — your business. Once you have decided in which direction you want to take your business, it will be much simpler to put together the plan of action. As you brace yourself to embark on this new venture, the key to setting yourself up for success is taking the time to complete a business plan, which we will discuss further in the next chapter.

Chapter 4

Preparing to Start Your Own Agency

The roadmap or blueprint for every successful business is a business plan. A business plan is meant to show you where your business vision is now, what the goals of the business are, and the steps that need to be taken in order to achieve the goals. A business plan is advisable whether you intend to use it as an internal document only or if you plan to use it as part of your application package when applying for business loans. Although a business plan acts as a guide for you to follow, nothing in the plan is set in stone. Instead, a business plan tends always to be a working plan or a work in progress. As you spend more time developing your skills, you might discover your desires have changed. The direction you thought the company might go could change altogether. Many factors can contribute to the changes, so having a plan helps you be proactive but also reactive, when necessary.

Resources to help you write your business plan are everywhere. Templates are available online at sites such as **www.score.org**, or you can search for business-plan templates using your favorite search engine. If you prefer to take a more professional approach to putting the business plan together, you also can work one-on-one with business plan writers or consultants, who will walk you through the entire process. *An adaptable business plan specific is included in the accompanying CD-ROM.*

Putting together the business plan on your own can be a learning tool in itself because it requires you to think through and make decisions on various aspects of your business. Other organizations that can help you through the process or provide you with business-plan models include:

- Small Business Association (SBA) (**www.sba.gov**): The Small Business Administration is an independent arm of the United States Government specifically dedicated to aiding, counseling, assisting, and protecting the interests of small businesses. The website offers a free course to guide you through writing your business plan.

- SCORE (**www.score.org**): SCORE or Counselors to America's Small Business is a network of business professionals who volunteer their time to encourage the development and growth of entrepreneurs. SCORE also has an online tutorial to help you put together your business plan.

Elements of a Business Plan

Business plans are your road map to success. The only way you can reach your goal of succeeding with your business is by having a plan. It is difficult at best to establish and operate a business when you do not quite know how to go about it — let alone, trying to accomplish it without a thorough assessment of what you want to accomplish, how you plan to go about it, and what financial support you need. As you prepare to undertake the enormous task of starting a new business, evaluate your situation as it stands today and visualize where you want to be three to five years from now. Working your way from today's standpoint to owning and operating a successful business, you must set goals to reach along the way, goals that will serve as benchmarks for you to check on your progress during the journey to success.

The most important and basic information to include in a business plan is:

- A statement of your business goals

- A description of the approach you will take to accomplish those goals

- A discussion about what potential problems you might encounter along the way and how you plan to address these problems

- An outline of the organizational structure of the business (as it is today and how you plan it to be)

- A statement about the capital you need to get started and to operate the business

Various formats and models are available for developing business plans. Even entire books are devoted to guiding you through the development of a business plan. However, before you constrain yourself to any one format, consider that a business plan should be as unique as the business for which it is being written. No two businesses are the same, and even though there might be some basic similarities, each business is as individual and unique as each person. For instance, a business plan for a collection agency will include a section on resources to stay up-to-date with federal laws such as Fair Debt Collection Practices Act (FDCPA) and Fair Credit Reporting Act (FCRA). Even though it is recommended that you follow the basic structure of commonly used templates, you should customize your business plan to fit your needs. A number of websites provide you with a variety of samples and templates that also can be used as references, such as **www.**

bplans.com, **www.nebs.com/nebsEcat/business_tools/bptemplate**, and **www.planmagic.com**, to name a few.

When writing your business plan, focus on its ultimate purpose and consider the many reasons why the plan is developed and its possible applications. For instance, if you do not have a loan proposal — essentially a condensed version of the business plan used by businesses to request financing when trying to secure financing for your business — business plans make great supporting documentation to attach to a loan application. Plans also are used as a means of introducing your business to a new market or presenting your business to a prospective business partner or investor. *A template of the following business plan, which follows the basic structure of a generic business plan and incorporates key elements of your business, is included on the accompanying CD-ROM.*

Parts of a Business Plan

When you begin a business plan, it is important to understand each part of your plan. Your business plan is divided into parts, with your mission statement and executive summary being the first. Before that, you will need a cover page that summarizes the contents of the packaged plan.

Cover page

The cover page should be laid out evenly with all the information centered on the page. Always write the name of your company in all capital letters in the upper half of the page. *Coming up with a name for your company will be discussed in Chapter 8.* Several line spaces down, write the title "Business Plan." Write your company's address, the contact person's name (your name), and the current date last. Each time you update your business plan, change the original date to the new date, so you know you are reviewing the most recent version.

Sample cover page

NAME OF COMPANY

Business Plan

Address
Contact Name
Date

Table of contents

The table of contents should tell the reader the main topics of your business plan. They should be listed as follows:

- Mission statement
- Executive summary
- Description of proposed business
- Management and staffing
- Market analysis
- Industry background
- Target market
- Product description
- Market approach strategy
- Marketing
- Operations
- Strengths and weaknesses
- Financial projections
- Conclusion
- Supporting documents

Body of the business plan

MISSION STATEMENT

A mission statement is a clear and precise purpose for your business. Ultimately, this mission statement is a beacon to guide you in the right direction. When writing your mission statement, you should consider three key elements: the purpose of your business, the services you provide, and a statement of your company's attitude toward your employees and customers. A well-written mission statement could be as short as one paragraph but should not be longer than two.

I. EXECUTIVE SUMMARY

The executive summary should be about one to two pages long. Even though the executive summary comes at the beginning of the plan, it is typically the last piece you write because it is a summary of all the information included in the plan. The executive summary should address your market, the purpose of the business, where the business location will be, and how the business will be managed. Write the executive summary in such a way that it will prompt the reader to look deeper into the business plan. It is a good idea to discuss the various elements of your business plan in the order you address them in the rest of the document.

II. DESCRIPTION OF PROPOSED BUSINESS

Describe in detail the purpose for which the business plan is being written. State what it is that you intend to accomplish. Describe your services and the role your business will play in the overall global market. Explain what makes your collection business different from your competitors. Clearly identify the goals and objectives of your business. The proposed business description section should average one to two pages long.

III. MANAGEMENT AND STAFFING

Clearly identifying the management team and any other staff that might be part of the everyday operations of the business will strengthen your business viability by demonstrating that the business will be well managed. Keep in mind that employees are a company's greatest asset. State who the owners of the business are, as well as other key employees with backgrounds in the collection industry. Identify the management talent you have on board (this may include yourself) as well as any others you might need in the future to expand your business. For instance, it might just be you when starting up; however, in your plans for expansion, you might think of incorporating someone well-versed in legal compliance. The management and staffing section of the plan could be as short as one paragraph, if you are the only employee, or it could be as long as one or two pages, depending on how many people you have or anticipate having as part of your staff.

IV. MARKET ANALYSIS

The market analysis section should thoroughly explain the target market. If you are new to the industry, do your research and include information you have acquired through research and data collection. Numerous sources of information are available, both online and through printed media, which can provide you with a wealth of knowledge about collection industries, geographic region information, and specific details on the types of clients you will be working with to collect on their accounts. This process adds validity to your presentation and better prepares you to answer any questions that might come up from the presentation. Essential elements to include in this section include your geographic area and a description of your services, a list and short description of your direct competitors, and your planned strategy and approach to the market. The market analysis element of your business plan should be one of the most comprehensive sections of the plan, and it can be several pages long, depending on the number of services and the market you intend to cover. In particular, the target market portion of this section alone easily can be two or three pages long.

Industry background

The collection industry is vast, so providing a comprehensive description of collection in the global market would be overwhelming. Instead, focus on the segment of the market you will be servicing. Include trends and statistics that reflect the direction the market is going and how you will fit into that movement. Discuss major changes that have taken place in the industry in the recent past, which will affect how you conduct business. Provide a general overview of your projected customer base, such as wholesalers or domestic consumers. Great sources to research online are U.S. Customs and Border Protection (**www.cbp.gov**), the World Trade Organization (**www.wto.org**), United States International Trade Commission (**www. usitc.gov**), and the International Trade Administration (**www.trade.gov**).

Target market

This is one of the largest sections of the business plan because you will be addressing key issues that will determine the volume of sales, and ultimately, the revenue that you will be able to generate for your business. The target market is who your customer, or groups of customers, will be. By this point, you already should have decided on the role you will take on; so, it is a good idea to narrow down your proposed customer base to a reasonable volume. If you try to spread your possibilities too thin, you may be wasting your time on efforts that will not pay off and end up missing some real opportunities. Identify the characteristics of the principal market you intend to target, such as demographics, market trends, and geographic location of the market.

Discuss what resources you used to find the information you needed on your target market. For example, state whether you used the World Trade Organization's website or U.S. Customs' statistical data. Elaborate on the size of your primary target market — your potential clients — by indicating the possible number of prospective customers, what their purchasing tendencies are in relation to the collection services you provide, the geographical location, and the forecasted market growth for that particular market segment. Expand your discussion to include the avenues you will use to reach your market. *Chapters 8 and 9 will discuss marketing and advertising techniques in more detail.* Include whether you plan to use the Internet, printed media, trade shows, and such. Trade shows are exhibitions organized with the purpose of providing a venue where companies can showcase their products and services. Explain the reasons why you feel confident your company will be able to compete effectively in the collection industry. Discuss your pricing strategies to be able to compete in the global market, such as discount structures in the form of bulk discounts or prompt payment discounts. Finally, you must address potential changes in trends that might favorably or negatively impact your target market.

Service description

Do not just describe your service — describe it as it will benefit or fill the needs of potential customers, and center your attention on where you have a clear advantage. Elaborate on the type of collection services that will be offered.

Market approach strategy

How do you anticipate entering the crowded collection market? Do you anticipate carving out a niche? Determining how to enter the market and what strategy to use will be critical for breaking into the market. *For further information on marketing strategies, please see Chapter 8.*

V. MARKETING STRATEGY

In order to operate a financially successful business, you not only must maintain a constant flow of income, but also boost your profits by increased sales. The best way to accomplish this is through an effective marketing program, such as promoting your products and services by advertising, attending trade shows, and establishing a presence on the Internet, to name a few. The marketing strategy element of the business plan identifies your current and potential customers, as well as the means you will use to advertise your business directly to them. The marketing-strategy portion of your business plan is likely to be several pages long — at least three to four pages — depending on how much detail you include in the plan. The marketing strategy section should include the following elements: products and services, pricing strategy, sales/distribution plan, and advertising and promotions plan.

Services

This section focuses on the uniqueness of your collection services and how your potential customers will benefit from them. Describe, in detail, the services your business provides, how the services are offered, and what makes your services unique and different from other collection businesses with the same services or similar services. Address the benefits of using your services instead of those of the competitors.

Pricing strategy

The pricing strategy segment is about determining how to price collection services in such a way that it will allow you to remain competitive while allowing you to make a reasonable profit. You will be better off making a reasonable profit rather than pricing yourself out of the market and losing money by pricing your services too high or not being able to turn a healthy profit because you price your services too low. Therefore, you must take extreme care when pricing your services. The most effective method of doing this is by gauging your costs, estimating the tangible benefits to your customers, and making a comparison of your services and prices to similar collection services in the market.

A good rule to follow is to set your price by taking into consideration how much the services cost you (or effort and time put into collecting a debt), and then add what you think would be a fair price for the benefits these services will provide to the customer. When you are determining your cost of services, you must consider all the costs, such as postage, the cost of labor and materials, selling costs, and administrative costs.

You should address why you feel the pricing of your services is so competitive in comparison to others. If your price is slightly higher than that of the competition, you need to justify why. It might be that you have more experience than your competitor or that you specialize in a niche your competitor does not. Perhaps your collection times are faster than your competitors'. In addition, it is noteworthy to point out the kind of return on investment (ROI) you anticipate to generate with the pricing strategy and set a specific time frame. ROI is a return ratio that compares the net benefits, in this case, of your services versus the total cost.

Sales and distribution

Now that you have determined how to price your services, it is time to think about how you are going to sell and promote your services. Describe the system you will use to obtain debt account information from clients, work through the debt list to try to collect on the debts, and bill your customers. Also, address what methods of payment you will accept from your customers, including credit terms and discounts. *Chapter 6 offers details on software programs you can use to implement these procedures.*

Advertising and promotion

Discuss how you plan to advertise your services through market-specific channels, such as direct mail. Promote your business to a specific market. One of your goals in this section is to break down what percentage of your advertising budget will be spent and on which forms of advertising. For instance, the cost of advertising through trade magazines, trade shows, and via an Internet differ significantly, and the return of your investment on each one of these might not be worth what you spend. Therefore, it is wise to evaluate carefully your advertising and promotion plans before putting them into effect. *For additional details about advertising for your business, see Chapter 9.*

VI. OPERATIONS

Under the operations section, all aspects of management are discussed. Concentrate your discussion on how to improve resources in operations and recovery methods, which will facilitate the success of the company. Remember that all of the information outlined in this section needs to be backed by realistic numbers, such as cost of office space, supplies, and equipment, as well as salaries and other costs for running your business. Also, discuss the current and proposed locations of the business, describing in detail any existing locations.

VII. STRENGTHS AND WEAKNESSES

As is the case in most industries, the competition in the collection business is tough because numerous business owners in the market are competing for the same prospects. Companies that focus on their strengths and work to overcome their weaknesses will get ahead of the game. In this section of the plan, elaborate on the particulars of your business that have enabled you, and will continue to enable you, to be successful. Discuss those things that set you apart and give you an advantage over your competitors, such as your particular geographic location, that you specialize in a very specific niche such as collecting debts for physical therapy centers, or maybe the fact that you are skilled in multiple languages, which allows you to work business deals in several countries or with various types of debtors.

There are no strengths without weaknesses, and as hard as it might be to face and deal with those weaknesses that could be holding you back, addressing them actually will help you either to overcome them or deal with them better. Remember that having weaknesses is not unique to your business because your competitors have weaknesses to deal with, too. Some weaknesses you might be dealing with at the time you are writing the business plan might be due to inexperience and limited exposure to the market, both of which can be overcome. Each of the weaknesses identified must be discussed in detail on how you plan to overcome the weakness or how you foresee ultimately eliminating it.

Although important, discussing strengths and weaknesses should not take way from other focal points of the business plan. Therefore, keep this section relatively short — no more than one page long.

VIII. FINANCIAL PROJECTIONS

Financial projections normally are derived from already existing historical financial information. Therefore, even though your goal in this section is to address financial projections for your business, you should include some historical financial data that will help support your projections. If you are preparing a business plan as part of your business startup process, historical financial data obviously will not be available, and working with estimates based on the performance of similar collection businesses is acceptable. If you are using the business plan as part of the application process for a loan, be sure to match your financial projections to the loan amount you are requesting.

When developing your financial projections, you must consider every possible expense, expected and unexpected, yet be conservative in your revenues. It is not critical that your actual revenues exceed the estimated amount; however, it is not a good situation when expenses are more than expected. Your projections should be addressed for the next three to five years, breaking down each year with the following information: forecasted income statements, cash flow statements, balance sheets, and capital expenditure budgets. Due to the nature of this section, you can anticipate it taking up several pages of your business plan, as you might want to include some graphs, in addition to the budget forms, to depict the information more clearly.

IX. CONCLUSION

The conclusion is a summation at the end of the business plan. Make use of this last opportunity to state your case wisely and highlight key issues discussed in the plan. Then wrap it up and close with a summary of your plans for the expansion and progress of your business. Use language to help the reader visualize what you will be able to accomplish and how successful your business will be should you receive the support you are requesting.

X. SUPPORTING DOCUMENTS

Attaching supporting documentation to your business plan will strengthen it and make it more valuable. However, do not overburden it with too many attachments; finding a balance is important. Before you start attaching documents, ask yourself if that particular piece of information will make a difference — if the answer is no, leave it out. Documents you should attach include:

- Copies of the business principals' résumés
- Tax returns and personal financial statements of the principals for the last three years
- A copy of licenses, certifications, and other relevant legal documents
- A copy of the lease or purchase agreement if you are leasing or buying space
- Copies of letters of intent from suppliers (if applicable)

Drawing up Compliance Plans for Your Business

A compliance plan is the general set of rules and policies the agency and employees must follow to prevent unwanted disasters such as lawsuits or bad publicity. Any person joining your agency, after reading your compliance plan, easily should be able to understand the policies of your agency and the consequences of not complying with the compliance plan.

As an agency owner, you are responsible for what goes on in your company. So, if employees break the law or avoid following policies, you could be facing possible lawsuits from clients, debtors, or employees. Furthermore, the compliance plan covers all departments within your company.

The Compliance Plan components

Introduction: Explain the general code of conduct for your agency. This might include internal issues, such as how to treat fellow coworkers, what not to include in email communications, phone etiquette, and harassment. Other things to consider for compliance plans include:

- Laws that govern the collection industry and where to find updates
- Procedures for reporting to the credit bureaus
- Procedures to protect company, consumer, and client critical information against identity theft
- Writing and updating collection letters
- General notices for internal communications and working with one another

Small agencies sometimes assign the compliance plan to the human resources manager. Larger firms might decide to hire a compliance officer to develop, oversee, train on, investigate incidents, and update procedures for compliance.

Compliance plan resources

Many companies offer guidance for developing your first compliance plan. Try visiting a few of the following online sites to see which one is best for your business:

- Cornerstone Support Inc. (**www.cornerstonesupport.com**): This company assists collection agencies to ensure they are in compliance with everything from the licensing the company is required to have to insurance and bonding requirements.

- The Association of Credit and Collection Professionals (**www.acainternational.org**): This association provides education and resources for creating a compliance plan for your business and to ensure that your business remains in compliance by providing you with updates on laws, regulations, and other industry news.

- National Association of Credit Management (**www.NACM.org**): This organization is dedicated to educating and informing credit and debt collection professionals and agencies to stay in compliance with laws and regulations for the industry.

Ways to Finance a Business

As stated earlier in this chapter, one of the primary purposes of a business plan is to use it as a tool to obtain financing for the business. When it comes to obtaining the money you need to start and operate the business, you have numerous options that extend beyond obtaining a bank loan or traditional business financing. Some of the sources of funding include:

- **Personal Savings** — Especially for sole business owners, the primary source for business financing comes from your own personal savings or the money of each of the business owners.

- **Borrow it** — Money can be borrowed from banks, financial institutions, family members, and friends.

- **Sell it** — Selling a part of your company to investors can provide needed capital, but sharing ownership has its drawbacks.

- **Pledge it** — Private or public business development grants are available based upon your ability and willingness to "give back" to the community.

- **Share it** — Find a sponsor (coach), employer, business, or individual who will subsidize your business with the goal of enhancing his or her financial gains.

Examining your business and discovering your entrepreneurial style are the first steps to finding the funding that matches your company's needs. When the need for money arises, entrepreneurs can become consumed by raising capital. Their judgment becomes clouded and their decision-making ability compromised. The cliché "the end justifies the means" is not always true. Your first step in exploring your financing options is to determine what you are willing to sacrifice and the most efficient and cost-effective way to obtain the money you need.

Available financial sources

The following sections outline the types of financing available to businesses. Making the decision to start or expand a small business opens up a variety of considerations and options. Many burgeoning companies spend far too much time chasing down funds from sources that do not mesh with their business and goals for the business. Finding the right financing options or the wrong financing options can draw the line between the success of your business and running into serious problems down the road.

Give it: Your personal investment

Investors and lenders tend to expect you to provide a significant amount of the capital necessary to launch or expand your business. When an entrepreneur puts assets on the line, it sends the message that he or she is committed to making the company a success, which also makes it easier to acquire supplemental funding from outside sources. (There are a few exceptions, such as seed-money programs created to assist economically disadvantaged at-risk individuals.) It is recommended that you have enough money put away in a savings account to cover all of your living expenses for a three-year period in case it takes this long for your business to start turning a profit.

Investing your money

Nearly 80 percent of entrepreneurs rely on personal savings to begin a new enterprise. Using personal savings secures the entrepreneur's control and ownership of the business. Because it is your money, no debt is incurred and future profits are not shared with investors.

Converting personal assets to business use is the same as giving your business cash. Not only will you avoid purchasing these assets, but you also will be able to depreciate them. Your accountant will set up the conversion and depreciation schedules. If you have an accountant — and if you do not, think about employing one — they can explain these terms further. Depreciation is used to describe any method used to determine the value left in an item. For many people, their greatest personal asset is their home.

Lines of credit, refinancing, and home equity loans often are used to gather up the seed money for launching a new business. Raising cash this way can be risky because it puts your home up as collateral for obtaining the loan. If you default on the loan, it can mean the loss of your home. Personal credit cards, signature loans, and loans against insurance policies and retirement accounts are other common ways of raising startup capital from personal assets you already own.

Home-equity loans

Before deciding a home-equity loan is a viable financing option, you first have to determine how much equity you have built up in your home. You can estimate this figure using one of a couple of different options. First, you can hire an appraiser, which can cost anywhere from $275 to over $500 to determine the market value of your home. You then need to subtract any existing mortgage balances from the value. The difference between these two numbers is the total amount of equity you have in the home. Another option for determining the market value of the home is to work with a real-estate agent. An agent can use the sales prices of comparable homes in your area to estimate the value of the home.

Two types of equity options exist. One is a home equity loan, which works similarly to a traditional mortgage. You receive the amount of the loan in

a lump sum and start paying interest on the loan amount right away. The second option is a home equity line of credit, which is a revolving line of credit that works like a credit card. You can access the money on the line, up to line amount, as you need it. You only pay interest on the outstanding balance. As you use and pay back the amount you use, the line is available for you to use again.

If you decide to access the equity in your home, fees might be associated with establishing the loan. Some of the fees you should be aware of include:

- **Appraisal fees** — The fee a professional appraiser charges to determine the market value of your home.

- **Origination fees** — The fee paid to the establishment or individual processing the loan. A lender charges this fee to process the loan.

- **Title fees** — Fees associated with conducting a title search on the home and/or renewing the title insurance policy to cover the new loan

- **Stamp duties** — Taxes applied to a legal document such as the deed

- **Arrangement fees** — The commitment fee payable to the lender of the loan in order to reserve the mortgage funds

- **Closing fees** — Costs incurred during the loan process that are paid at the end of the transaction

- **Early payoff fee** — Fees that can be required if you pay off the loan early, typically within the first five years of acquiring the loan

If you own your home outright, you can refinance without staking all the equity you have in your home, which leaves room for future refinancing should something go wrong. If you own 20 percent or less in equity, by no means should you ever consider borrowing against that. The funds you gain will be minimal, and the second lender will not hesitate to foreclose should trouble arise. To determine feasibility of a home equity loan, follow these steps:

1. Get your home appraised. If the value has increased, you might own more equity than you think.

2. Figure out exactly how much you still owe on your mortgage.

3. Take the appraisal valuation and subtract your debt to determine the amount of equity.

4. Figure out your percentage by dividing your equity amount by the valuation amount. If it is less than 50 percent, you should find a different source of capital for your business.

5. If your equity is more than 50 percent, you might be in business. Now is the time to get loan quotes.

6. Figure out how your business plan will be affected by this cash infusion, and make projections for how long it will take for the loan to be paid off.

For example, if the market value of your home is $200,000 and your first mortgage balance is only $100,000, then you only owe 50 percent of the value of the home. This means that you have equity built up in your home that you can access to help pay for the startup or operating expenses of the business. As an added bonus, the interest you pay on a mortgage for a primary residence is fully tax deductible. Check with your tax adviser to verify this for your personal financial situation.

Pay down the principal balance of the debt in order to get out of debt faster and regain the equity on your home.

Leveraging your credit

Leveraging your personal credit worthiness is another way to support your business. Because a new business does not have established credit or a credit history, you might be able to leverage your personal credit by guaranteeing the business loan or credit account. Talk with your attorney about personal liability issues for any business debts you acquire. Part of this protection depends on the type of legal entity you establish for the business, such as corporation over a sole proprietorship.

Borrow it: Loans to repay

Borrowing money for business can save the business or be its downfall. When looking at various types of loans, consider such issues as collateral required, interest rates, and repayment terms. **Collateral** is the promise of a specific piece of property to a lender to facilitate repayment. **Interest rates** are the rates at which the borrow pays for the use of funds he or she borrows from a lender. The terms a borrower agrees to when the loan is acquired are the **repayment terms**.

> **WARNING:** If you ever hear anyone use the word **usury,** be careful. The word originally meant charging interest on a loan, but today it is used to describe an unlawful rise in interest charged on a loan or charging an excessive interest rate that is drastically higher than the market rate.

Loans from family and friends

Asking for help from those closest to you can be another smart move when looking for capital. Because you already have a relationship with friends and family, there are no questions of trust, and a willingness to help already exists.

Interest-free or low-interest loans from relatives or friends can help a startup business gain important supplemental capital without having to take out a bank loan or relinquish control and profits of the business to investors.

When considering these investors, ask yourself five questions:

1. Will this person be able to ride out the highs and lows without extensive panicking?
2. Does this person understand the risks and benefits?
3. Will this person want to take control or become problematic?
4. Would a failure ruin your relationship?
5. Does this person bring something to the table, besides cash, that can benefit you and the company?

Lines of credit

Tempting sources of short-term borrowing for small businesses are microloans. These alternative loans are often safer and have lower interest rates. They can help fill the gap between expenditures incurred while acquiring debt accounts to collect on and actually collecting the debt payments.

Lines of credit are useful for making sure payroll is met and that the short-term operating costs are covered during the gap.

Sell it: Shared ownership

Investors are a type of owner, which means you must be willing to "sell" a portion of your business and future profits in return for an investor providing you with the money you need up front to start the business or to expand it. Some investors are active participants in daily operations, while others act more as silent partners. Silent investors put the money up for the business based on a solid business plan, but they do not get involved in the daily operations of the business.

Summary

Once you decide to start a collection business, you have numerous steps ahead of you to get the business together before you can announce you are open for business. Licensing, zoning, bonding, certifications, and financing are some of the major issues you must address when getting ready to launch your collection business. Now that you are equipped with the tools to begin planning for the success of your business, the next chapter, Chapter 5 guides you through the legal aspects of establishing your new business. You will learn how to start your business off in good legal standing.

The Legal Standing of Your New Business

fter you have decided you want to start your business, it is time to set yourself up as a recognizable entity for government and legal purposes. This means going beyond the creative name you have made up and backing up the name with the appropriate documentation, filing, or identifications to become a valid business.

Determining the Legal Structure of Your Business

Deciding which legal structure you would like to build your business under will be the backbone of your operation. The legal structure of your business sets the platform for your everyday operations, as it will influence the way you proceed with financial, tax, and legal issues — just to name a few. It even will play a part in how you name your company, as you will be adding

Inc., Co., LLC, and such at the end of the name to specify what type of entity you have chosen for your business. The business entity you choose also dictates what type of documents need to be filed with the different governmental agencies, and how much and what type of documentation you will need to make accessible for public scrutiny, as well as how you operate your business. To assist you in determining how you want to operate your business, a description of the different legal structures is provided as follows, along with sample documents you may need to file with state and federal agencies, depending on where you live.

Business entity chart

Use the following chart to help you determine the legal structure of your business:

Legal entity	Costs involved	Number of owners	Paperwork	Tax implications	Liability issues
Sole proprietorship	Local fees assessed for registering business; generally run between $25 and $100	One	Local licenses and registrations; assumed name registration	Owner is responsible for all personal and business taxes.	Owner is personally liable for all financial and legal transactions.
Partnership	Local fees assessed for registering business; generally between $25 and $100	Two or more	Partnership agreement	Business income passes through to partners and is taxed at the individual level only.	Partners are personally liable for all financial and legal transactions, including those of the other partners.

Legal entity	Costs involved	Number of owners	Paperwork	Tax implications	Liability issues
LLC	Filing fees for articles of incorporation; generally between $100 and $800, depending on the state	One or more	Articles of Organization; operating agreement	Business income passes through to owners and is taxed at the individual level only.	Owners are protected from liability; company carries all liability regarding financial and legal transactions.
Corporation	Varies with each state, can range from $100 to $500	One or more; must designate directors and officers	Articles of Incorporation to be filed with state; quarterly and annual report requirements; annual meeting reports	Corporation is taxed as a legal entity; income earned from business is taxed at individual level.	Owners are protected from liability; company carries all liability regarding financial and legal transactions.

Becoming a Small Business

A small business is a company that is privately owned and operated with fewer than 500 employees. You will be joining more than 27.5 million other small businesses in the United States, according to the Small Business Administration (SBA). Small companies represent 99.7 percent of all employer firms in the country and contribute more than 45 percent of the total U.S. private payroll. More than half are home-based. Franchises make up 2 percent.

Of those 27.5 million small U.S. businesses, the SBA states that 552,600 new companies first opened for business in 2009. During the same period, 660,900 closed up shop. However, seven out of ten newly opened companies remain in business two years and half after the first five years. The odds are with startups that have owners working hard and that care about the company.

CASE STUDY:
OWNING AN AGENCY

Joel Lackey
National Credit Systems, president
www.nationalcreditsystems.com
(404) 629-9595

The responsibilities of being a collection representative cannot overshadow those of the president of the company. Owning your own collection agency can be overwhelming because, not only must you understand the inner workings of your agency, but you must also be able to enforce policies for both your employees and your clients.

Joel Lackey, the president of National Credit Systems, has been in the collection industry since 1991. He said the most challenging parts of his job are dealing with ridiculous lawsuits, such as debtors suing creditors and denying that the debt is theirs even though they have been receiving bill statements and collection letters at their address for years and never disputed the matter until the debtor winds up in court. The second most challenging thing to deal with is adhering to licensing requirements. The company sometimes must deal with a customer's unrealistic expectations of what their business actually does and it, sometimes, becomes his job to speak with disgruntled customers. "To overcome this, the agency takes the time to explain the processes so they [the clients] can understand," Lackey said.

Although Lackey deals with many hardships on a daily bases, he is confident in his employees and their ability to handle these difficult situations. "There is no substitute for a skilled, intelligent collection agent who can explain the debt and its many different components clearly to a debtor," he said. National Credit Systems specializes in apartment debt, which means that representatives must deal with many different elements including concessions, attorney fees, and even property damage. This also requires representatives to be very knowledgeable on all fronts of the business.

Lackey's company handles its own collection letters, whereas many other agencies have professional writers produce these. Lackey makes sure his employees are experts in their field, so they are able to write their own letters, but everything is still approved by the company's attorney.

As the president of your agency, you are called upon to make executive decisions, so it is very important that you are confident in your abilities, able to work well under pressure, and "you never give up," Lackey said.

Sole proprietorship

Sole proprietorship is the most prevalent type of legal structure adopted by startup or small businesses, and it is the easiest to put into operation.

It is a type of business owned and operated by one owner, and it is not set up as any kind of corporation. Therefore, you will have absolute control of all operations. Under a sole proprietorship, you own 100 percent of the business, its assets, and its liabilities. Some of the disadvantages are that you are wholly responsible for securing all monetary backing, and you are ultimately responsible for any legal actions against your business. However, it has some great advantages, such as being relatively inexpensive to set up, and with the exception of a couple of extra tax forms, there is no requirement to file complicated tax returns in addition to your own personal tax returns. Also, as a sole proprietor, you can operate under your own name or you can choose to conduct business under a fictitious name. Most business owners who start small begin their operations as sole proprietors and then evaluate a change later as the business grows, expands, and changes.

General partnership

A partnership is almost as easy to establish as a sole proprietorship, with a few exceptions. In a partnership, all profits and losses are shared between or among the partners. In a partnership, not all partners necessarily have equal ownership of the business. Normally, the extent of financial contributions toward the business determines the percentage of each partner's ownership. This percentage relates to sharing the organization's revenues as well as its financial and legal liabilities. One key difference between a partnership and a sole proprietorship is that the business does not cease to exist with the death of a partner. Under such circumstances, the deceased partner's share either can be taken over by a new partner, or the partnership can be reorganized to accommodate the change. In either case, the business is able to continue without much disruption.

Although not all entrepreneurs benefit from turning their sole proprietorship businesses to partnerships, some thrive when incorporating partners into the business. In such instances, the business benefits significantly from the knowledge and expertise each partner contributes toward the overall operation of the business. As your business grows, it might be advantageous for you to come together in a partnership with someone who is knowledgeable in the collection field and will be able to contribute toward the expansion of the operation. Sometimes, as a sole proprietorship grows, the needs of the company outgrow the knowledge and capabilities of the single owner and require the input of someone who has the knowledge and experience necessary to take the company to its next level.

When establishing a partnership, it is in the best interest of all partners involved to have an attorney develop a partnership agreement. Partnership agreements are simple legal documents that normally include information such as the name and purpose of the partnership, the legal address of the business, how long the partnership is intended to last, and the names of the partners. It also addresses each partner's contribution both professionally and financially and how profits and losses will be distributed. A partnership agreement also needs to disclose how changes in the organization will be addressed, such as death of a partner, the addition of a new partner, or the selling of one partner's interest to another individual. The agreement ultimately must address how the assets and liabilities will be distributed, should the partnership dissolve.

Limited liability company

A limited liability company (LLC), often wrongly referred to as limited liability corporation, is not quite a corporation, yet is much more than a partnership. An LLC encompasses features found in the legal structure of corporations and partnerships, which allows the owners — called members in the case of an LLC — to enjoy the same liability protection of a corporation and the recordkeeping flexibility of a partnership, such as not having to keep meeting minutes or records. In an LLC, the members are not personally liable for the debts incurred for and by the company, and profits can be distributed as deemed appropriate by its members. In addition, all expenses, losses, and profits of the company flow through the business to each member, who ultimately would pay either business taxes or personal taxes — and not both on the same income.

LLCs are a comparatively recent type of legal structure, with the first one being established in Wyoming in 1977. It was not until 1988, when the Internal Revenue Service (IRS) ruled that the LLC business structure would be treated as a partnership for tax purposes, that other states followed by enacting their own statutes establishing the LLC form of business. These companies are now allowed in all 50 states, and although they are easier to establish than a corporation, it requires a little more legal paperwork than a sole proprietorship.

An LLC would be most appropriate for a business that is not quite large enough to warrant assuming the expenses incurred in becoming a corporation or being responsible for the recordkeeping involved in operating as such. Yet, the extent of its operations requires a better legal and financial shelter for its members.

Regulations and procedures affecting the formation of LLCs differ from state to state, and they can be found on the Internet in your state's "corporations" section of the secretary of state's office website. A list of the states and the corresponding section of the secretary of state's office that handles LLCs, corporations, and such is included in the corporations section of this chapter.

Two main documents normally are filed when establishing an LLC. One is an operating agreement, which addresses issues, such as the management and structure of the business, the distribution of profit and loss, the method of how members will vote, and how changes in the organizational structure will be handled. The operating agreement is not required by every state.

Articles of Organization, however, are required by every state, and the required form is generally available for download from your state's website. The purpose of the Articles of Organization is to establish your business legally by registering with your state. It must contain, at a minimum, the following information:

- The limited liability company's name and the address of the principal place of business
- The purpose of the LLC
- The name and address of the LLC's registered agent (the person who is authorized to physically accept delivery of legal documents for the company)
- The name of the manager or managing members of the company
- An effective date for the company and signature

ARTICLE I — Name
The name and purpose of the Limited Liability Company is:

Fictitious Name: ABC Collection Agency, LLC
Purpose: To conduct…

ARTICLE II — Address
The mailing address and street address of the principal office of the Limited Liability Company is:

Street Address: 1 Collection Drive, Suite 5D
Recovery City, FL 32839

Mailing Address: P.O. Box 1235
Recovery City, FL 32839

ARTICLE III — Registered Agent, Registered Office, and Registered Agent's Signature
The name and the Florida street address of the registered agent are:

John Doe
5678 New Company Lane
Beautiful City, FL 33003

Having been named as registered agent and to accept service of process for the above stated Limited Liability Company at the place designated in this certificate, I hereby accept the appointment as registered agent and agree to act in this capacity. I further agree to comply with the provisions of all statues relating to the proper and complete performance of my duties, and I am familiar with and accept the obligations of my position as a registered agent as provided for in Chapter 608, Florida Statutes.

_____
Registered Agent's Signature

ARTICLE IV — Manager(s) or Managing Member(s)

Title	**Name & Address**
"MGR" = Manager	
"MGRM" = Managing Member	
MGR	Jane Doe
	234 Manager Street
	Beautiful City, FL 33003

MGRM

Jim Unknown
789 Managing Member Drive
Beautiful City, FL 33003

ARTICLE V — Effective Date
The effective date of this Florida Limited Liability Company shall be January 1, 2014.

REQUIRED SIGNATURE:

_____
Signature of a member or an authorized representative of a member

Corporations

Corporations are the most formal type of all the legal business structures discussed so far. A corporation can be established as a public or a private corporation. A public corporation, with which most of us are familiar, is owned by its shareholders (also known as stockholders) and is public because anyone can buy stocks in the company through public stock exchanges. Shareholders are owners of the corporation through the ownership of shares or stocks, which represent a financial interest in the company. Not all corporations start as public corporations selling shares in the open market. They might actually begin as individually owned businesses that grow to the point where selling stocks in the open market is the most financially feasible business move for the organization. However, openly trading your company's shares diminishes your control over it by spreading the decision-making to stockholders or shareholders and a board of directors. Some of the most familiar household names, such as the Tupperware° Brands Corporation and The Sports Authority° Inc., are public corporations.

A private corporation is owned and managed by a few individuals who normally are involved in the day-to-day decision-making and operations of the company. If you own a relatively small business but still wish to run it as a corporation, a private corporation legal structure would be the most beneficial form for you as a business owner because it allows you to stay closely involved in the operation and management. Even as your business grows, you can continue to operate as a private corporation. There are no rules for having to change over to a public corporation once your business reaches a certain size. The key is in the retention of your ability to closely manage and operate the corporation. For instance, some of the large companies that we are familiar with and tend to assume are public corporations happen to be private corporations, such as Domino's* Pizza, L.L. Bean, and Mary Kay* cosmetics.

Whether private or public, a corporation is its own legal entity capable of entering into binding contracts and being held directly liable in any legal issues. Its finances are not directly tied to anyone's personal finances, and taxes are addressed separately from its owners. These are only some of the many advantages to operating your business in the form of a corporation. However, forming a corporation is no easy task, and not all business operations lend themselves to this type of setup. The process can be lengthy and put a strain on your budget due to all the legwork and legal paperwork involved. In addition to the startup costs, there are additional ongoing maintenance costs, as well as legal and financial reporting requirements not found in partnerships or sole proprietorships.

To establish your corporation legally, it must be registered with the state in which the business is created by filing Articles of Incorporation. Filing fees, information to be included, and its actual format vary from state to state. However, some of the information most commonly required by states is listed as follows:

- Name of the corporation
- Address of the registered office
- Purpose of the corporation
- Duration of the corporation
- Number of shares the corporation will issue

- Duties of the board of directors
- Status of the shareholders, such as quantity of shares and responsibilities
- Stipulation for the dissolution of the corporation
- Names of the incorporator(s) of the organization
- Statement attesting to the accuracy of the information contained therein
- Signature line and date

For instance, Alabama's format for filing the Articles of Incorporation can be accessed through the state's Secretary of State Corporate Division website. The website contains instructions for filling out and submitting the document along with corresponding filing fees.

STATE OF ALABAMA
DOMESTIC FOR-PROFIT CORPORATION
ARTICLES OF INCORPORATION GUIDELINES

INSTRUCTIONS:

STEP 1: CONTACT THE OFFICE OF THE SECRETARY OF STATE AT (334) 242-5324 TO RESERVE A CORPORATE NAME.

STEP 2: TO INCORPORATE, FILE THE ORIGINAL, TWO COPIES OF THE ARTICLES OF INCORPORATION, AND THE CERTIFICATE OF NAME.

RESERVATION IN THE COUNTY WHERE THE CORPORATION'S REGISTERED OFFICE IS LOCATED.

THE SECRETARY OF STATE'S FILING FEE IS $40. PLEASE CONTACT THE JUDGE OF PROBATE TO VERIFY FILING FEES.

PURSUANT TO THE PROVISIONS OF THE ALABAMA BUSINESS CORPORATION ACT, THE UNDERSIGNED HEREBY ADOPTS THE FOLLOWING ARTICLES OF INCORPORATION.

Article I. The name of the corporation:

Article II. The duration of the corporation is "perpetual" unless otherwise stated.

Article III. The corporation has been organized for the following purpose(s):

Article IV. The number of shares, which the corporation shall have the authority to issue, is_____.

Article V. The street address (NO P.O. BOX) of the registered office:

_____

_____, and the name of the registered agent at that office:

_____.

Article VI. The name(s) and address(es) of the Director(s):

Article VII. The name(s) and address(es) of the Incorporator(s):

Type or Print Name of Incorporator

Signature of Incorporator

Rev. 7/03

Any provision that is not inconsistent with the law for the regulation of the internal affairs of the corporation or for the restriction of the transfer of shares may be added.

IN WITNESS THEREOF, the undersigned incorporator executed these Articles of Incorporation on this the _____ day of _____, 20_____.

Printed Name and Business Address of Person Preparing this Document:

Sometimes, finding the correct office within the state government's structure that best applies to your needs can be a challenge. The same office might have a different name in different states. In this case, the name of the office that provides services to businesses and corporations might be called Division of Corporations in one state, Business Services in another, Business Formation and Registration in another, and so forth. Therefore, to save you time and frustration while trying to establish a business, here is a shortcut so you can reach the appropriate office for filing the Articles of Incorporation without having to search though the maze of governmental agencies in your state:

State	Secretary of State's Office
Alabama	Corporations Division
Alaska	Corporations, Businesses, and Professional Licensing
Arizona	Corporation Commission
Arkansas	Business / Commercial Services
California	Business Portal
Colorado	Business Center
Connecticut	Commercial Recording Division
Delaware	Division of Corporations
Florida	Division of Corporations
Georgia	Corporations Division
Hawaii	Business Registration Division
Idaho	Business Entities Division
Illinois	Business Services Department
Indiana	Corporations Division
Iowa	Business Services Division
Kansas	Business Entities
Kentucky	Corporations
Louisiana	Corporations Section
Maine	Division of Corporations
Maryland	Secretary of State
Massachusetts	Corporations Division
Michigan	Business Portal
Minnesota	Business Services
Mississippi	Business Services
Missouri	Business Portal
Montana	Business Services
Nebraska	Business Services
Nevada	Commercial Recordings Division
New Hampshire	Corporation Division
New Jersey	Business Formation and Registration
New Mexico	Corporations Bureau
New York	Division of Corporations

State	Secretary of State's Office
North Carolina	Corporate Filings
North Dakota	Business registrations
Ohio	Business Services
Oklahoma	Business Filing Department
Oregon	Corporation Division
Pennsylvania	Corporation Bureau
Rhode Island	Corporations Division
South Carolina	Business Filings
South Dakota	Corporations
Tennessee	Division of Business Services
Texas	Corporations Section
Utah	Division of Corporations and Commercial Code
Vermont	Corporations
Virginia	Business Information Center
West Virginia	Business Organizations
Washington	Corporations
Washington, D.C.	Corporations Division
Wisconsin	Corporations
Wyoming	Corporations Division

S corporation

An S corporation is a form of legal structure; under IRS regulations designed for small businesses, "S corporation" means small business corporation. Until the inception of the limited liability company form of business structure, forming S corporations was the only choice available to small business owners that offered some form of limited liability protection from creditors, yet afforded them with the many benefits a partnership provides. Operating under S corporation status results in the company being taxed close to how a partnership or sole proprietor would be taxed rather than being taxed like a corporation.

Operating under the S corporation legal structure, the shareholders' taxes are impacted directly by the business's profit or loss. Any profits or losses the company might experience in any one year are passed through to the shareholders who in turn must report them as part of their own income tax returns. According to the IRS, shareholders must pay taxes on the profits the business realized for that year in proportion to the stock they own.

In order to organize as an S corporation and qualify as such under the Internal Revenue Service regulations, the following requirements must be met:

- It cannot have more than 100 shareholders.
- Shareholders must be U.S. citizens or residents.
- All shareholders must approve operating under the S corporation legal structure.
- It must be able to meet the requirements for an S corporation the entire year.

In additional, Form 253, "Election of Small Business Corporation," must be filed with the IRS within the first 75 days of the corporation's fiscal year.

Electing to operate under S corporation status is not effective for every business; however, it has proven to be beneficial for a number of companies through many years of operation. Because of the significant role S corporations play in the U.S. economy, The S Corporation Association of America was established in 1996 to serve as a lobbying force in Washington and protect the small and family-owned businesses from too much taxation and government mandates. Membership in the association is composed of S corporations, both big and small, from throughout the nation. This includes companies such as the Sumner Group, headquartered in St. Louis, Missouri. The Sumner Group is one of the largest independently owned office equipment dealerships in the nation.

Obtaining an Employer Identification Number (EIN)

All employers, partnerships, and corporations must have an Employer Identification Number, also known as a Federal Tax Identification Number. You must obtain your EIN from the Internal Revenue Service before you conduct any business transactions or hire any employees. The IRS uses the EIN to identify the tax accounts of employers, certain sole proprietorships, corporations, and partnerships. The EIN is used on all tax forms and other licenses. To obtain one of these, fill out Form SS-4, obtainable from the IRS website (**www.irs.gov/businesses/small**) and by clicking on "Small Business Forms and Publications." There is no charge. If you are in a hurry to get your number, you can get an EIN assigned to you by telephone, at (800) 829-4933.

Also, request the following publications, or you can download them via the Internet at **www.irs.gov**:

1. Publication #15, circular "Employer's Tax Guide"

2. Several copies of Form W-4, "Employer Withholding Allowance Certificate." Each new employee must fill out one of these forms.

3. Publication 334, "Tax Guide for Small Businesses"

4. "All about O.S.H.A." and "O.S.H.A. Handbook for Small Businesses." Depending on the number of employees you have, you will be subject to certain regulations from this agency. Their address is: O.S.H.A., U.S. Department of Labor, Washington, D.C. 20210, **http://osha.gov**.

5. "Handy Reference Guide to the Fair Labor Act." Contact: Department of Labor, Washington, D.C. 20210, **www.dol.gov**.

Each of these publications provides more information on the various aspects of running a small business.

Opening a Bank Account

Taking the time to meet with a bank representative when you go to open a business checking account is time well spent, and you will be surprised by the many services available and the sound financial advice you can receive from bank officials. Discuss with a representative your plans for starting up your business and where you foresee your business going in the future. This information will allow the bank representative to advise you as to what type of business checking account best suits your needs. He or she also can provide you with information regarding services provided by the bank, which could benefit you during the early stages of your business and in the future. This is also a good time to find out about the bank's policy on a business line of credit account, which is beneficial to have when starting a new venture. A line of credit account is an arrangement through a financial institution whereby the bank extends a specified amount of unsecured credit to the borrower.

In order to establish a business checking account, most financial institutions require a copy of the state's certificate of fictitious name filing from a partnership or sole proprietor, or an affidavit to that effect. An affidavit is a written declaration sworn to be true and made under oath before someone legally authorized to administer an oath. To open a business checking account for a corporation, most banks will require a copy of the Articles of Incorporation, an affidavit attesting to the actual existence of the company, and the Employer Identification Number acquired from the IRS.

If your collection agency decides to enter into the international market, the first element you need to look for when you are in the market for a financial institution is a bank with a strong international department. A banking institution with an international department — such as Bank of America, Wells Fargo, Global Connect, and Regions Bank, to name a few — are able to handle and process specialized transactions, such as foreign exchange payments and letters of credit. Letters of credit are documents used by financial institutions to guarantee payments on behalf of their customers — the buyer of the goods — thereby facilitating the business transactions between the two parties. In addition, you would want the bank to provide other services such as speed in handling transactions, electronic banking, a strong but flexible credit policy, and a good, solid relationship with other financial institutions overseas.

Hiring an Attorney for Your Business

Most businesses have attorneys on staff or on retainer. Initially, your agency might not be able to hire or retain an attorney, but it is highly recommended to build a relationship with one. The collection industry can be very rewarding, but as with any other industry, there is lot of room for error when you are ignorant of laws that govern you locally and nationally. Your attorney can review your collection letters to ensure they are in line with the FDCPA guidelines, draw up important documents such as collection agreements, draw up and modify legal documents, advise you on business decisions, and represent you in court should any need arise. There are attorneys that specifically represent collection agencies, and there are general business attorneys who also can help your business stand on proper legal grounds. If you can afford it, it is better for a collection agency to hire an attorney that specializes in the industry. Because of their specialization, these attorneys tend to charge a higher fee than a general attorney, but the extra money is worth knowing that everything is taken care of and nothing falls through the cracks. A good way to find an attorney is to ask around; find out which attorneys other agencies are using. Another way to find an attorney is by searching the yellow pages. Many attorneys do not charge for the initial consultation, so it is feasible for you to meet with multiple lawyers to find out which one you are comfortable with and which ones fit within your budget. If you find an attorney you like but are not able to retain, ask the attorney if he or she is willing to work with you on an as-needed basis. For instance, you might want your attorney to draw up legal documents one month, and you only pay for the services used at that time. Later, you might need him or her to modify a previously written contract. Find out if the attorney requires a retainer or how he or she charges for services.

Prepaid legal services

Another option is to consider prepaid legal services. Prepaid legal services allow individuals and businesses to pay a nominal monthly fee for access to legal services. This fee is paid whether you use the legal services or not. Numerous prepaid legal plans exist, so conduct research to find which service best fits your budget and business needs. Make sure you understand exactly what you are receiving in return for paying the monthly fees. Also, ask if additional fees are charged for additional services, such as court representation.

Resources for finding an attorney

- FindLaw® (**www.findlaw.com**)

- American Bar Association (**www.abanet.org**)
- Attorneys.com (**www.attorneys.com**)
- Superpages™ (**www.superpages.com**)

Summary

When you are starting up a business venture, it is sound practice to seek the advice of business professionals in their fields of expertise.

The information contained in this book serves as only an informational basis to help you to understand the overarching legalities of starting and operating a collection business. You should speak with a legal professional before making any important decisions that will affect you legally. You should establish a strong working relationship with a well-established financial institution as an essential component of the financial success of your business.

Once you have your business in good legal standing, you then can move on to putting the other pieces of the puzzle together to move toward opening your doors for business. In Chapter 6, you will uncover some of the accounting and collection software programs available to you for use in your business that maximizes the effectiveness of your business.

Accounting and Collection Software Program

A company's accounting software serves as the financial backbone or foundation of the business. Typically, any additional software used has a way of being integrated into the accounting software — not the other way around.

Accounting Software

There are hosts of accounting software programs from which to choose. You should consider the amount of work you have, types of clients you have, and the types of accounts you will be working to choose the best accounting software program for your business. The price of the software depends on the features of the program and the number of licensed users that need access to the program.

Although this is not a comprehensive list, a few of the most popular software programs and features include:

- **QuickBooks** — QuickBooks is a popular software program for small businesses. It is easy to learn and simple to use. There are many versions of QuickBooks, but most versions permit businesses to print checks, pay bills, manage payroll and taxes, email estimates and invoices, accept debit and credit cards, and organize and back up documents. For more information on the software, visit **www.quickbooks.intuit.com**.

- **SAP** — SAP is more than an accounting software program; it is a business management software typically used in large businesses. The SAP software helps integrate departments and practices of multiple departments within a business, including information technology (IT), finance, product development, operations, sales, marketing, and customer service. The tools available in this program are strategic and might require you to receive training. The great thing about using SAP is that you can customize the software to fit the specific needs of your business. For more information, visit **www.SAP.com**.

- **Microsoft Dynamics˚ GP** — Once known as Great Plains Dynamics, Microsoft Dynamics GP is a software program similar to SAP in that it helps integrate all levels and departments of a business. Most important, it offers an accounting system that is easy to learn and use. Dynamics is a great program if you are working with overseas clients because the program allows you to complete financial transactions in multiple currencies without worrying about changing exchange rates.

- **SYSPRO˜** — SYSPRO is another great accounting software program for both large and small businesses that allows your business to decide which functions work best with your company. There are a number of accounting functions, including accounts payable, accounts receivable, cashbook, and activity-based accounting. You can find more information by visiting **http://americas.syspro. com**.

- **Sage Peachtree** — With Peachtree, you can accept credit cards and help alleviate the hassle of year-end closing, which is closing out your accounting books for the year and getting ready for tax season, an imperative part of running a business. The Sage Peachtree software creates the reports you need to give to your accountant for tax filing purposes. To learn more about Peachtree; visit **www. peachtree.com**.

Collection Software

Collection software can be quite expensive; however, it is well worth the investment, considering it is the basis of a collection business. The heart of what you do involves tracking debtors and their payments. Collection software can be sophisticated and sometimes complicated. Make sure you do your research to find out which software is the easiest for you and your company to use. Look at the details or subgroups of the types of reporting offered. The main reporting groups might consist of transactions claims and lists. A subgroup of a transaction would be payments; the subgroup of a claim may be statement of account; a subgroup of list might be attorney. Obviously, many other subgroups will fit in each of these reporting modules. Preferably, you want a representative of the collection software to provide you with a product demonstration online or in person. You might want to involve your IT person in the demonstration as well, to ensure the collection software will be compatible with your computer systems and any other software programs you use in the business.

Some of the collection software programs available include:

- **eCollections** — eCollections is an award-winning collection management software from Sentinel Development Solutions. The software is easy to use and includes a lot of high-end features, predictive dialers, and modules. For more information, send email to sales@eCollections.com, or visit **www.eCollections.com**.

- **WebAR** — WebAR is a Web-based computing multiple function accounts receivable management platform and collection system. If you prefer not to install another software program on your computers, this program instead allows you to access the program online. As long as you have Internet access, you have access to the program. Learn more about this software by visiting **www.interprose.com**.

- **PIMS & eStrats** — This is another web-based software program for the collection industry that is also a portfolio analysis system. The software is great for small, medium, or large businesses and runs on the widely used Microsoft environment. For more information contact info@pimsware.com or visit **http://pimsware.com**.

- **WinDebt° XL** — This is accounts receivable software program that offers a PowerQue Desktop feature. PowerQue Desktop allows you to assign specific accounts to a specific collector. You can learn more by emailing info@windebt.com or visiting **www.windebt.com**.

- **Totality** — This software program is for startup collection agencies. It is specifically designed for small to mid-sized agencies. This software is efficient and easy to learn. For more information contact info@TotalitySoftware.com or visit **www.totalitysoftware.com**.

The list above is to help you begin your search. Ask the software providers for a few references and have a list of questions ready to ask. A few important questions include:

1. How well does the software provider respond to and rectify any technical issues?

2. Does the software provider offer an in-depth, easy to understand training program?

3. For Web-based programs, how often do you have issues with long periods of downtime?

4. Are the modules easy to access and understand?

5. Is each viewing page easy to view? Do your eyes easily navigate the page without being confused?

Summary

Collection agencies that leverage technology tend to be more efficient than agencies that do not adopt the technology and software programs readily available to the industry. Because collection software programs offer easy data entry and retrieval and a way to protect sensitive information, using one of these programs serves to better organize the collection process. Missing a date to call a debtor to collect a payment might cause you to stop receiving any more payments on the accounts. With these types of software programs, alerts can be set up and assigned to the correct collection representative to avoid allowing items to fall through the cracks. Accounting and collection software programs are two very different things. Accounting software serves the purpose of tracking accounts, purchasing, preparing taxes, cash applications, payroll, and more depending on the software.

When considering any kind of software for your new agency, it is a good idea to talk to colleagues in the industry to find out what programs others are using and the pros and cons of each. Consider first, what you will need for your company because each software provider will have different applications to help you run your business. You will have to speak to one of the provider's sales representatives to review your specific needs. It is not a good idea to research collection software programs online only. Speak to a professional.

Chapter 7

Staffing Your Agency

As your agency grows, in order to expand the company in a prosperous direction, you will have to consider hiring employees. Staffing an agency must not be considered lightly. When running any business, the human capital is an invaluable asset. Your agency most likely will be considered small, but the compilation below provides information on small, medium, and large agencies. There are variances from one agency to another; however, the positions below are important to consider. The salaries included are based upon the low-end of the 2011 Salary Guide from Robert Half International.

Large		Medium		Small	
Credit manager/ supervisor	$63,500	Credit manager/ supervisor	$50,250	Credit manager/ supervisor	$42,500
Assistant credit manager	$49,250	Assistant credit manager	$40,750	Assistant credit manager	$36,000
Credit collections analyst	$39,750	Credit/collections clerk	$29,250	Credit/collections clerk	$28,000

Large		Medium		Small	
Credit/collections clerk	$31,750				

The salaries noted are based on research provided. There are many things to consider when deciding on a salary for a new employee. Each candidate's experience, skills, and salary history must be looked at individually. Other issues to consider when deciding on salaries include the market rate for your area.

Deciding What Type of Candidate to Interview

Before actually interviewing candidates, the agency must decide what position needs to be filled and develop a job description. Because your company is uniquely different from a candidate's prior employer, develop a training

manual in advance so each new employee knows exactly what is expected of him or her and can have a smooth transition into the new position. Not setting objectives in advance is the reason for many failed employee/ employer relationships within all industries. If an employee has no vision of what he or she is supposed to be doing, he or she might not complete the tasks at all or might not take the most efficient route for completing the tasks.

In a job description, tell potential candidates about the position, provide a clear description of it, list tasks and responsibilities, and spell out the experience/skills needed to execute the job. If desired, a brief description about the agency is acceptable. The following is a basic job description for a credit-and-collection clerk:

Position:
Collection agency seeks experienced credit and collection clerk with previous work in a fast-paced collection environment.

Description:
- Oversee collection for 100 accounts, including tracking and updating system of conversations and payment plans
- Use collection and accounting software applications for analyzing account detail and strategizing work assignments
- Familiar with current state and federal laws pertaining to collection and maintaining compliance
- Receive and process customer payments via mail, fax, email, or phone
- Listen to customers to understand their situations and help them make plans to pay off debts
- Use logic and resources to quickly solve problems
- Execute research using court files, skip tracing, and online queries

Required Skills

- Minimum of two years collection experience
- Proficiency using computers, phone, printer, and fax
- Written and verbal communication skills
- Ability to remain calm and composed even under pressure
- Good negotiation and mediation abilities
- Excellent listening skills
- Experience working with accounting and collection software

Education

High school diploma or equivalent

Posting the position online

One place where you can post your ad is on Craigslist (**www.craigslist. org**), which is a free classified website on which users can post local ads for various products and services, including job openings. Craigslist is such a popular site that it is typical to be inundated with both legitimate and junk emails. It requires you to do some sifting and sorting so you can identify qualified candidates. You also have the option to post jobs on career websites such as Monster", Career Builder", and Simply Hired". The fees for posting online vary, but a typical range might be from $99 to $300. The following list describes things to consider before posting a job:

- Posting location: locally or nationally?
- Posting validity/duration: How long will the posting or ad last?
- Available posting discounts
- Additional services bought from provider

Preparing to Interview Candidates

Like many jobs, collection can be stressful with the added effort of having to listen to and work around the issues and concerns of debtors. So, be cautious about hiring candidates who are retainable — ones who fit the profile to work in a collection environment. Some traits to consider include:

- Drive
- Motivation
- Poise and control
- Able to work under pressure

CASE STUDY: HIRING REPRESENTATIVES FOR YOUR COMPANY

Tom Haag
State Collection Services Inc., owner
2509 S Sloughton Rd.
Madison, WI 53716
tomh@stcol.com
www.statecollectionservice.com

Tom Haag, who has more than 40 years experience in the collection industry, took over his father's failing agency and began making a profit in just six months. State Collection Services Inc.'s largest segment is commercial and consumer collection, with health care being the second largest.

With a growing agency, Haag had to come up with a way to weed out candidates when he began hiring employees. There were distinctive traits that he assessed would be profitable for his agency, and he asked questions accordingly. "The ability to communicate is paramount when looking for employees," he says. "When a candidate is asked tough and surprising questions, showing their ability to communicate and deal with the unexpected, it shows that they could be a valuable asset." Haag also looks for candidates that have maintained stable employment, have equally stable work histories, and have progressed within their careers.

Haag said the most important skill for a collection agency representative to have is the ability to think through tough situations and come up with appropriate solutions. "Common sense would be at the top of the list of skills to have," he says.

When hiring employees, it is important to have examples of businesses to emulate and look up to. Every business, no matter how large or small, was in the planning stages of their company at one time — as you are now.

Testing Candidates

The interview process has become complicated for candidates and employers. Candidates are waiting longer to receive job offers, and companies are taking longer to extend them. Some of the wait is due to prequalification testing and grading. If an employee lies or exaggerates on his or her résumé or during the interview about what he or she can do, it eventually will show up in the performance. The goal is to get it right the first time, and this can be done with some prequalification testing, if you can afford to do so. Some recommended testing includes:

- Computer and software experience
- Accounts receivable
- General math skills

Retaining Quality Employees

Do not allow a good employee to get away from you. It is too hard to find high-quality and reliable people. Make sure you have an incentive plan in place to reward top-tier performance. A company can use several methods, such as:

- Create a positive work environment that rewards top performers, such as offering competitive salaries and benefits.

- Implement a scorecard or performance metrics to monitor individual and departmental success.

- Be willing to promote quality employees to positions throughout the company to help advance their careers. They might have to change jobs but will continue to be an invaluable resource to your company.

Discriminatory Practices

Under Title VII, the ADA, and the ADEA, it is illegal to discriminate in any aspect of employment, including:

- Hiring and firing
- Compensation, assignment, or classification of employees
- Transfer, promotion, layoff, or recall
- Job advertisements
- Recruitment
- Testing
- Use of company facilities
- Training and apprenticeship programs
- Fringe benefits
- Pay, retirement plans, and disability leave
- Other terms and conditions of employment

Discriminatory practices under these laws include:

- Harassment based on race, color, religion, sex, national origin, disability, or age

- Retaliation against an individual for filing a charge of discrimination, participating in an investigation, or opposing discriminatory practices

- Employment decisions based on stereotypes or assumptions about the abilities, traits, or performance of individuals of a certain sex, race, age, religion, or ethnic group, or individuals with disabilities

- Denying employment opportunities to a person because of marriage to, or association with, an individual of a particular race, religion, national origin, or an individual with a disability. Title VII also prohibits discrimination because of participation in schools or places of worship associated with a particular racial, ethnic, or religious group.

Employers are required to post notices to all employees advising them of their rights under the laws that EEOC enforces and their right to be free from retaliation. Such notices must be accessible to persons with visual or other disabilities that affect reading.

These guidelines should be followed by all business people, even small, startup businesses like yours. Once you select a person to hire, you will need to set up a personnel file for him or her, prepare the appropriate government paperwork for tax withholding, and implement other new-hire policies. If you are not sure what is required, your accountant, your state tax officer, or your local chamber of commerce can point you in the right direction.

Application of Federal Law to Employers

A number of factors might cause an employer to be covered by a federal employment law. These include the number of employees employed by a business; whether an employer is a private entity or a branch of federal, state, or local government; and the type of industry an employer is in.

The following chart shows how the number of workers a company employs determines whether a specific federal statute applies to the business:

Number of Employees	Applicable Statute
100	WARN — Worker Adjustment and Retraining Notification Act
50	FMLA — Family Medical Leave Act

Number of Employees	Applicable Statute
20	ADEA — Age Discrimination in Employment Act·
20	COBRA — Consolidated Omnibus Benefits Reconciliation Act
20	OWBPA — Older Workers Benefit Protection Act
15	ADA — American with Disabilities Act
15	GINA — Genetic Information Nondiscrimination Act
15	Title VII of the Civil Rights Act of 1964
15	PDA — Pregnancy Discrimination Act
1	EPPA — Employee Polygraph Protection Act
1	EPA — Equal Pay Act
1	FRCA — Fair Credit Reporting Act
1	FLSA — Fair Labor Standards Act
1	IRCA — Immigration Reform and Control Act
1	OSHA — Occupational Safety and Health Act
1	PRWORA — Personal Responsibility and Work Opportunity Reconciliation Act
1	USERRA — Uniform Services Employment and Reemployment Rights Act

Creating an Ethical Environment

The most effective fraud deterrent is a corporate culture that does not tolerate fraud. Creating an ethical culture in the workplace is a process that takes time, investment, and continual education. For an ethical culture to become established, both management and employees must be committed to it and willing to live by it every day.

Ethics policy or code of conduct

Every organization should have a formal ethics policy, not only because it deters fraud, but also because it legally supports efforts to enforce ethical conduct in the workplace. Employees who have read and signed a formal ethics policy cannot claim they were unaware their conduct was unacceptable. Recommended codes of conduct for various types of organizations are commercially available, but every organization should tailor its own ethics policy to suit its business and its needs. A good ethics policy is simple and easy to understand, addresses general conduct, and offers a few examples to explain how the code might be applied. It should not contain myriad rules to cover specific situations or threats such as "violators will be prosecuted to the full extent of the law." In a legal trial of a fraud perpetrator, it is the judge and not the company who decides the sentence. An ethics policy or code of conduct should cover:

- **General conduct at work:** Explain that ethical and honest behavior is expected of all employees, and they are expected to act in the best interests of the company.

- **Conflicts of interest:** Employees might not understand what does and does not constitute a conflict of interest, so some simple examples are appropriate.

- **Confidentiality:** Company policy on the sharing of information among employees and departments or with people outside the company

- **Relationships with vendors and customers:** Company policy regarding doing business with a relative, friend, or personal acquaintance

- **Gifts:** Policy regarding the types and amounts of gifts that might be accepted or given by employees during the course of doing business

- **Entertainment:** The types of entertainment activities considered appropriate for vendors and customers and that will be accepted on expense accounts

- **Relationships with the media:** Company policy regarding who should communicate with the media about company affairs

- **Use of the organization's assets for personal purposes:** This section should cover personal use of the Internet while at work and use of copy machines, telephones, and company vehicles

- **Procedure for reporting unethical behavior:** Employees should be encouraged to report any ethical violation, large or small. This section should explain how and to whom reports should be submitted.

- **Consequences of unethical behavior:** Discipline options should be communicated clearly and consistently enforced.

An ethics policy will not be effective if it is handed to each new employee and then forgotten. The ethics policy should be reviewed with employees every year, ideally as part of an anti-fraud education program.

Building Effective Teams

Team building has always been an important part of any business. There are even business sectors geared to providing independent contractors who work alone with access to team members to help brainstorm ideas and overcome hurdles. It is one thing to reach out to different websites, organizations, associations, and other resources to acquire insight into the best way to handle problems or run your business. On the other hand, the best resources are found right in your business — the very people who work with, for, and around you. Even before hiring a new candidate, let them know that you have a team-oriented environment, and everyone is expected to participate in improving and sustaining the business. This is not to take away from individual responsibility or accountability within specific positions.

What is a team?

A group of people does not necessarily constitute a team. Other factors are involved when talking about teams. Teams do not just happen but are created, introduced, and implemented into a business structure as an important business practice. When a person does not understand their role in a team, he or she stands out like a sore thumb and causes frustration for the rest of the group. A successful team consists of members that exhibit the following characteristics:

- Cohesiveness
- Mutual accountability
- Leadership and synergy
- Collaboration
- Commitment toward a common goal

Cross-functional teams

It is rare to hear the phrase, "that's not in my job description," in the corporate environment anymore. Employees understand that the most effective and successful work day comes by preparing the next person or department for success. The mentality of cross training and preparedness to help the customer at any cost is imbedded in the minds of employees. Your employees should not be required to perform a job function that is not a part of their responsibilities. The goal, however, is to allow teams to know what other teams are doing and responsible for and to encourage small steps to ensure a smooth transition from one process to the next in the work environment.

Tips for a successful team

After you have established your teams, the next step is to establish best practices, goals, and responsibilities for each team. Take time to deal with the most common obstacles that employers or team leaders face. By working on these team qualities, you will build a team that can react effectively and immediately, to any situation. Some of these obstacles include:

- **Low morale:** Offer encouragement and help team members get back on track.
- **Lack of direction:** Set clear, attainable goals with deadline.
- **Lack of knowledge or skills:** Offer training and seminars as often as possible.
- **Lack of cohesiveness:** Change or switch members between teams.

Summary

Collection representatives work in a high-stress environment. At the same time, it is important that they perform their jobs according to the standards set by your company. In order to find and retain the best employees, use the tips from this chapter to place effective job ads, interview qualified candidates, and hire, train, and retain these qualified employees for years to come. Although you are not a psychiatrist, you will have to have minimal empathy because your human capital is the most important asset to your business. Avoid getting involved in an employee's personal issues, but instead offer resources, such as an employee assistance program (EAP), which is a mental-health counseling program for employees used as a money-saving way to provide insurance coverage for mental health problems.

Chapter 8

Marketing — Developing Your Company's Image

The term 'marketing' is often interchangeable with the terms 'advertising' and 'public relations'. Advertising and public relations are both tools that fall under the umbrella of marketing. Marketing is the effective creation, promotion, distribution, and selling of a brand. In this book, advertising and public relations are described as two ways you can promote your collection services. Consider the fact that marketing encompasses both science and art and covers everything you need to do to get your services in front of potential clients. Marketing has a lot to do with telling the story of how your services benefit the clients in a way that stands above your competition. The most effective way to accomplish this is to create a consistent overall image.

Image is everything. The collection industry has an extremely damaged image to date, and because of the negative connotation associated with collection, it is important to develop a positive brand image for your business.

Do some brainstorming as to what image you would like to present to the public, and most importantly, your target market, which will be discussed in more detail later on in this chapter.

Branding is Perception

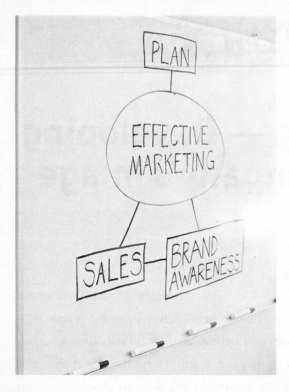

Many companies create a brand based on how they want their customers to feel and connect with the company and services. Unfortunately, it is not always about how a company wants their customers to feel. In reality, a brand is really about how current and potential customers perceive it to be. Finding the balance between how you want your brand to be perceived and how it actually is perceived is the key to successful branding.

When brand perception is off balance in a for-profit business situation, it can be even more important because it might mean the difference between running a profitable collection agency and having to close the business forever.

Three Ways to Balance the Brand with Audience Perception

1. Create and write a mission statement for the company that is understood and memorable.

2. Survey potential and current clients to see what they think the company does and what services it offers. If this matches the purpose of the company, the brand and brand perception are in balance. If not, adjustments need to be made so the balance is restored.

3. Segment messaging with the audience. No matter what type of collection agency you have, chances are you have several different market segments you cater to — for one, you have clients that are in a specific industry. When creating a brand and messaging, make sure this aligns with the audience you are targeting. For example, the messages you send to your potential customers for a credit card company may be vastly different from those in the medical industry.

Customer perception is everything when it comes to branding. You can hire the most expensive branding company in the world to design your logo and create a brand for your business, but if the company brand and customer perception do not match, it is all just a waste of time and money.

How to brand

Branding helps you create a universal image that the public identifies instantaneously. For instance, you want to present your company as a collection agency that has a peaceful presence but, at the same time, gets the job done. You might want to create a tag line or slogan such as "The peaceful alternative." The colors you choose for your brand, website, and other promotional materials might be earth tones such as brown, peach, orange, grass green, and golden yellow. Be sure to stick with a consistent color palate to establish a firm brand. In this example, these warm colors create a sense of peace and warmth and will help your debtors associate the warmth of the colors with your business.

Taking this example one step further, you could create a logo with blurred edges that does not have an abrupt structure. To create peace, the logo might be more circular or oval rather than a sharp triangle that creates a sense of force. Now, if a company wants or needs to create this image, then they should use triangular-based logos. Your logo is displayed prominently on official documents such as letters, envelopes, and even as signatures in email correspondence. Many logos are used as a substitute for the company name, especially if the name is exceptionally lengthy or difficult to pronounce.

Another way of creating your brand is the development of a universal way of treating customers and the public. When hiring new employees, inform them that you are maintaining a peaceful environment and instruct them how you expect them to conduct themselves while working with debtors. This does not take away from your employees being aggressive in recovering funds on behalf of your client. Aggressive business practices can be married successfully to a peaceful brand.

Overall, your main goal is to come up with something cohesive and consistent to reflect your company's purpose. Image development is important because it is how your clients see you, which can either gain business or take away business. A brand can benefit the operation of your business by:

- Building an environment for customer loyalty
- Increasing product, service, or company credibility
- Creating a cohesive, consistent tone and message
- Touching people in an emotionally effective way
- Making your company stand out from the competition
- Positioning your company to develop and acquire market share

Deciding on a name

The name you select for the company is very important and, if selected properly, helps people remember your brand. If you are working as a freelancer with the legal standing as a sole proprietor, you typically use your own name for your business. This has to be done in order to file taxes using a Social Security number. When selecting a name other than your own, consider the words you are using and if they have negative connotations or different meanings in other languages. Collection companies want to make their names represent exactly what they do so that there is no confusion about it; thus, choosing a name that can only have one meaning is the best way to go. The following lists of words are good to include in a collection business name. Keep in mind that you want people to be able to identify what you do by reading your name.

Great words to include in a collection business name:

- Agency
- Asset recovery
- Billing & collection
- Collection
- Control
- Credit
- Financial
- Management
- Merchant services
- Network
- Professional
- Receivables
- Recovery
- Resolution
- Services
- Solutions
- Specialty

Do not call it quits after creating one name, but instead, decide on a couple of names because your first choice already might be in use by another company. Each state only allows one company to operate by that name, but you might want to avoid choosing the same name as an existing company, even if it is operating in a different state. This is because the other company might have a poor reputation or because customers might be confused as to which company is which if the names are the same or too similar. This is even more imperative in a world where more businesses are national and even global than ever before. With the Internet, it is extremely easy for customers in California to locate a collection agency in New Jersey, for example. So, if you have the same name as an agency in New Jersey, you still will be associated with them and their image — be it good or bad. Go online to your state's site for fictitious names to verify that the name is not already in use and to register your name. Being the first to register the name provides you with ownership and a legal standing in case another business tries to use it in the future. If someone tries to use your name without authorization or vice versa, a lawsuit can be filed, which can incur court costs and time that can be avoided by doing some research up front.

Tips for Developing Your Brand

Brainstorm with colleagues and advisers to decide how you want to present your business and what it will stand for. Perform this step with care, and consider the values and guarantees the company should exhibit. These things are all important to your client, and even debtors will do research to find out what you stand for. Think about the number of times you purchase a product and immediately look for the guarantee or warranty. This is the same type of thing — your brand is your warranty. These things show the public how serious you are about gaining, and keeping, their respect and business.

- **Values:** Your company values will promote the sound functioning of the business and to strengthen the fabric of it.

o   Some examples of values to consider for a collection agency would be in helping clients' recover receivables to ensure the clients' financial stability. Your prospective and current clients will appreciate your concern for them.

- **Mission Statement:** Consider your purpose of existence. This is what your mission statement presents to the public. A mission statement can be short or long but typically incorporates the moral, ethical, and social standings of the business. In addition, it explains what services you are offering to the target market.

o   Example collection mission statement: ABC Collection Agency provides services to retail businesses by providing aggressive and legally acceptable collection tactics to recover unpaid debt. We exhibit the highest level of ethics and ensure debtors are treated with respect and dignity.

- Vision Statement: A company without a vision will perish. The company vision should explain to the principals, investors, and employees the destination of the business.

o   Your agency's vision statement might be to become the premiere agency in the Southeast region of the United States and recover debt for Fortune 100 retailers.

Developing a logo

The logo is a symbol that companies, organizations, and sometimes individuals use to identify themselves. Logos are very important to the overall brand. Marketing companies and graphic designers are excellent resources to help you develop your company logo. However, most collection company logos are kept very simple with few distractions. The goal is not take too much away from the name; let the name do the talking. In this industry, the name will be more powerful than the logo. Before selecting a logo or meeting with a graphic designer, look at a few of your competitors' logos to get some ideas.

Incorporating trademarks into the marketing package

A trademark is a word, symbol, phrase, sound, or smell that represents the product to the public. Many trademarked logos and symbols are widely recognized, such as the McDonald's golden arches, the Pepsi logo, and the MasterCard logo. Examples of trademarked sounds are the chimes for the broadcast station NBC and the Yahoo yodel. Your brand name, logo, or other symbol(s) that differentiate your service from a competitor's all can be trademarked. To be protected, the mark must either be used in commerce or registered with the intent to use it. Although using the item is sufficient to establish trademark rights, registration with the U.S. Patent and Trademark Office (USPTO) can strengthen trademark enforcement efforts. The letters TM in superscript next to a word, brand, or logo is sufficient to designate the word, brand, or logo is trademarked. The TM is the designation for a nonregistered trademark. A trademark that has been

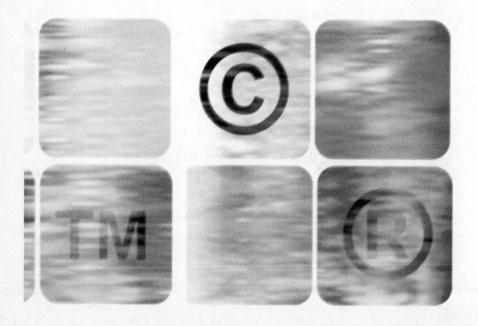

registered with the USPTO is designated with the R with a circle around it (®). Use of the ® for a nonregistered trademark could interfere with the right of its creator to register the mark subsequently.

Professional trademark searches can cost between $300 and $1,200. Nevertheless, you can avoid these charges by using the Internet and conducting some of your own research. Search registered and pending trademarks at the U.S. Patent and Trademark Office (USPTO) website (**www.uspto. gov**) and use the Trademark Electronic Search System (TESS). You can access this by going to the middle column, selecting "Search Marks," and then going to the "Basic Word Mark Search (New User)." From there, you type in the name you want to use, and click "Submit Query." Be certain that the "Field" term is on "Combined Word Mark." For a comprehensive search, be certain to perform the following:

- Enter all names that are phonetically similar to your company — these names can cause conflicts in trademark use. For example, if you want to name your company Netflicks, you should enter Netflix as well.

- Enter the singular and the plural spellings of your company's proposed name.

- If your proposed name has more than one word, enter each word separately.

- Use "wild card" search terms, such as the asterisk (*) to broaden your search. For example, if you are searching for Netflicks, you can enter Netfli*, to search for similar names that began with the same six letters.

Be advised that trademark searches are not foolproof. Searches reveal only those names that are registered. Unregistered business names might be in use as well. They would be considered valid even if they did not show up in the USPTO database. Consequently, after searching there, you should search the Internet for the proposed name. This should reveal any current users of your proposed name. If you have reached this stage without discovering any conflicting trademarks or service marks, you should then search the secretary of state's records for existing corporate names. Most states offer free searches of existing corporate names, generally through their Office of the Secretary of State.

If your name passes the previous tests, you might want to reserve it. This step is not necessary but is recommended as you move to the planning and development stages of your new business. Most states offer a reservation service where you file a short name reservation form with the secretary of state, but a fee for this service varies according to the state. When you have finalized your name, make sure you have an appropriate corporate suffix to make the public aware of your limited liability protection, if you have decided to incorporate your business. Use the following suffixes as appropriate for your business name:

- Corporation or Corp.
- Incorporated or Inc.
- Limited or Ltd. In some states this suffix can be confused with a "limited partnership" or "limited liability corporation"

Weaving the Brand Together

Once you determine the look and feel you want to use to represent your personal and company brand, the most important aspect of branding is weaving it into every aspect of your collection business. Branding encompasses everything that is internal and external with your company, so whether it is a memo that goes around to the internal employees of the business or an email that you are sending out to the client list, the brand standards apply. Some of the items you need to consider when applying the business brand include:

- Company logo
- Business cards
- Email signature
- Letterhead
- Brochures
- Marketing kit
- Website
- Blog
- Mailing envelopes
- Promotional items, such as pens, magnets, notepads, and Koozies
- Proposals
- Client agreements or contracts

Understanding Your Target Market and Obtaining a Share

Trying to serve and please too many people at one time is a recipe for disaster. A realistic entrepreneur and business owner defines a segment of the collection industry that he or she can serve confidently and efficiently. Collection companies do not have to try to take on all types of collection. You might want to focus on retail, child support, or health care recovery services as your niche, or target market. Doing too many things could lead to doing each thing only partially right.

Target markets are not just based on the types of collection you choose to pursue, however. Markets encompass business types, size, location, or even average amount of collection. The more specific the target market is, the more directly you can focus your advertising and public relations efforts. Promoting a business is expensive; so imagine not having specified a target market and spending capital on reaching businesses that cannot or will not use your services. It is more effective and feasible to market aggressively to a specified few. Before a potential investor gives you money or a bank extends a loan to you, one of the primary sections of the business plan they will read is the target market section. The specific target market you are promoting to is defined in the marketing plan portion of your business plan.

While researching a target business, a few things to find out include:

- Current collection agency on record
- Current services used if any
- Satisfaction with agency on record
- Number of accounts they have in collection

Scouting the Competition

Once you have defined your target market, your next goal is to find out where they are located. If you have the capital to hire a market research company to assist with these efforts, this would be beneficial. Another option to help you discover where your clients might be is to using the Yellow Pages to look for companies that work in the type of collection you wish to specialize in. Your local chambers of commerce and industry associations are great sources to locate and network with potential clients. Joining social networking sites and business chat rooms are great alternatives. Within these forums, you can find out where your potential clients are and what issues they currently have surrounding debt and payments.

After you have identified where your market is and developed a database of contacts, the next step is to find out which one of your competitors is currently serving them. The best way to do this is to ask them via phone or survey. While talking with them, find out how satisfied the potential client is with your competitor. Look for the following things to help your business measure up to your competitors:

- Weaknesses of your competitor: Knowing your competitor's weaknesses is beneficial when trying to appeal to a new client. Your personal presentation and advertising can then be geared at how well you can serve the potential client in this area.

o   For example, if your competitor has had a hard time with skip tracing, which is conducting research to follow the trail of a debtor to find out where they are living or working when debtors have moved out of state, you can boldly emphasize your skip-tracing resources and success rate in finding debtors who have left the state. Even if your company is brand new, if you have any experience with debt collections, you can use that as a strength in your promotions as well.

- Strengths of your competitor: A competitor's strengths are hard to overcome and should not be attempted. It is better for you to represent your collection agency with having comparable strengths as the competitor, if this is true. If this is not true, try to woo the potential client with a strength you have in another area.

o   For example, if a competitor has a high success rate for recovering commercial debt over $10,000 and you cannot make this claim, focus on the fact that you have valuable resources and will diligently try to collect, but the client pays nothing if you do not.

Summary

Image selection is vitally important for your business because it can mean the number of clientele you acquire in your first few months of operation, which ultimately can determine how successful your agency is. You want to be aware of the name you select for your new agency as well because this also can determine how many clients recruit your agency to handle their collection.

When you finally do select your agency's name, logo, and brand, you will have a better idea of the market demographic you want to target. The longevity of your agency is determined by your ability to target the appropriate people with your innovative marketing. This will help you discover the other agencies you will have to compete with for clients. An important way to discover your competition is to ask. However, do not stop there; dig deeper to secure information on the issues they have with the competitor. And if they are willing to discuss pricing with you, document this information as well. From this, you will have a plan for developing your marketing, pricing, and promotional strategy.

Chapter 9

Promoting Your Agency and Acquiring Clients

You might have the superior collection business in your niche or in your geographic region, but if your ideal customers do not know it exists, it is all for naught. This is where marketing and promoting your collection business come into play. Before the Internet playing such an integral role in promoting a business, collection agencies relied heavily on local advertising, advertising in media products that reached their niche, and good, word-of-mouth advertising. Although collection businesses still rely on their local advertisements and word-of-mouth advertising, these businesses also must integrate online advertising and promotional efforts with their offline efforts for the most effective and efficient way to promote and grow the business. Ideally, you should find some kind of combination of online and offline marketing efforts, but especially when starting out, these efforts really have to fall within the budget you have for promoting your business. Typically, a new startup company has limited resources, so it is a good idea to learn effective ways to market your business that fall within your budget using no- or low-cost options.

When marketing a new business, consider advertising and public relations. **Advertising** is a form of communication used to promote a brand and persuade the intended audience to purchase a specific service, in this case collection services. **Public relations** (or PR) is a field concerned with bringing awareness of the company image, brand, and services to the intended audience but in more of an indirect way than advertising. You always have the option to hire advertising and public relations firms to handle all of this work for you. The drawback is that this can be an expensive way to promote and bring awareness to your business. As a more econom-

ical route, you either can choose to hire freelancers such as writers, graphic designers, and public relations specialists to do it for you or to do it on your own. Many of these freelancers have advertising and public relations backgrounds, so they can provide you with a high-level quality of service but at a lower cost than some of the big firms. Although conducting these functions yourself is inexpensive, or free, it does take time — time that might be better spent conducting and managing the day-to-day work of your business.

Creating Your Marketing Plan

The marketing plan is one of the biggest sections of the business plan. Because the marketing plan plays such a vital role in running your business, however, the rest of this chapter provides more details on putting the marketing plan together and specifies the types of marketing you might engage to promote and advertise your business.

As is the case with most business decisions you make, you should start by setting a marketing budget. Once you know how much money you have to spend on promoting and marketing your business, it is much easier to identify the different options available and then put together a mix of these options to figure out what methods of promotions work best for your collection agency.

Methods of promotion to consider

Unfortunately, there is no magic potion every collection business can use that produces the perfect results. Marketing requires you to test different forms of advertising and to then test the results of each effort. As you find one effort to be effective, you then have to add in the next form of advertising you want to test to see how it works out.

Some of the advertising methods include:
- Newspaper/magazine ads
- Postcards
- Promotional items
- Radio/TV commercials
- Fliers

CASE STUDY:
ADVERTISING FOR
YOUR AGENCY

Andrea Behrens
Nevada Association Services Inc.
6224 W. Desert Inn Road
Las Vegas, NV 89146
www.nas-inc.com

When beginning a business, it is extremely important to get your company's name in the spotlight and choose a specific demographic, or else you will have no clientele to keep your business afloat. Andrea Behrens, who works for Nevada Association Services Inc., does collection for the homeowners' association and says that because they work with specific kinds of clients, their advertising must reflect that. "Mass market approaches are not effective for us, so we do not advertise in typical outlets. For us, direct mail to our own list and advertising in community newspapers have proven to be most effective," says Behrens. Community involvement also has been a great way the company has become well-known in the area.

Another key to their successful advertising has been agency press releases. "We do press releases on company news and constantly promote our executives as subject matter experts on topics such as collection, homeowners' association, and foreclosures," she says. It also helps that the CEO of the company is very articulate and has a good sense of humor, which has made him a media magnet and sought-after interviewee. "He even cohosts a television show all about homeowner association issues," she says.

In additional, client acquisition techniques, such as free seminars at high-end restaurants, have been very successful. "We also partner with colleagues in our industry, such as attorneys, to team up on seminars," said Behrens.

The Internet also has been a lucrative outlet for advertising, and Behrens said it is important to keep the information you relay fresh and new. You cannot keep stale information on your website, for example, or people never will return. You must stay in front of your target, "or someone else will." Behrens says. Social networking sites, such as Facebook and Twitter, have become major staples for businesses trying to target specific people for services. "We were the first in our industry's area to offer clients status reports online. We also invested heavily in social media and launched our own Facebook page," she says. In the near future, they plan to explore Twitter, blogging, and YouTube.

The most important factors to remember when you are trying to execute marketing for your new collection agency are to have extensive knowledge about the industry and hire experts who know what they are doing.

Using Public Relations

Public relations is the process of using the media to help promote a business or movement. Public relations tends to be free publicity for your business because it is typically won by using avenues that do not cost the business money but can be highly effectively in getting the word out. In short, public relations can be one of the most cost-effective ways to promote your business. The cost associated with using public relations to promote your business probably will only be the time investment it takes.

Types of public relations

The following list outlines a few options available to promote a business; they are some of the most advantageous. Figure out what type of message about the agency you want to send out to prospects. Before getting to this stage, you should brainstorm to decide which target market your company will go after — again, this is information you pinned down when you wrote your business plan. It is better to try to capture a set target market than to spend excessive time and funds trying to reach every business.

- Press releases
- Articles
- Speaking engagements

- Newsletters
- Social/business networking
- Blogging
- Social media

The press release is the start of any public relations campaign. It is a document used to communicate with the media: television, radio, newspapers, magazines, and web editors or bloggers. Media outlets use the information in a press release to generate stories of interest for their readers or followers. Members of the media do not take kindly to receiving frivolous or improperly directed information on a consistent basis, but they do want to be made aware of newsworthy events, topics, or information that is relevant and of interest to readers, watchers, or followers. Knowing when to write a press release is the key to success. Avoid writing a release just to write a release — find a timely reason. Some good reasons to write about a business include:

- A grand opening or reopening
- Launching of new services or programs
- New partnerships
- Company recognition via awards
- Hiring new executive-level employees
- Newsworthy events related to your clients, business, or industry

Sample press release

FOR IMMEDIATE RELEASE

ABC Collection agency
Contact: Marylyn Doe
Phone: (800) 000-0000
Email: email@abccollectionagency.com

ABC Collection Agency Partners with Onpoint Skip Tracing to offer state-of-the art Search Services

Orlando, FL (June 1, 2014) — ABC Collection Agency is now an Onpoint Skip Tracing provider.

Onpoint provides an all-in-one, top-tier skip tracing that covers basic, legal, and international business or individual searches. Onpoint has been awarded for its quality and results worldwide and has a 96-percent success rate. All clients of ABC Company will be able to take advantage of this unique resource that is only available to professional collection agencies.

"We integrated the Onpoint system to our services, and we have already seen an increase in our collection results," said CEO of ABC Collection Agency Marilyn Doe. The implementation of the new service has not caused a substantial increase in the fees the agency charges its clients. ABC Collection Agency is always looking for new resources to assist with the recovery of its clients' past and current receivables.

ABC Collection Agency is an Orlando-based collection agency that offers collection resources to retailers and banks. It has been in business for eight years. ABC Collection Agency has offices in Orlando and Jacksonville.

Onpoint Skip Tracing is located in New Jersey and has been in business since 2006. The Onpoint software developed for collection agencies was recently upgraded in 2014, giving clients access to resources needed to search for debtors at the tip of their fingers. Onpoint always has customer service representatives and investigators on hand to assist collection agencies with skip tracing.

Resources for submitting a press release

Submitting a press release to the media is a simple process. There are multiple fee-based and free services for distributing a press release to multiple outlets at once. Another option is to submit the press release yourself to individual outlets. The goal is to know which media outlets and publications your target audience follows and reads. Submitting a press release to a magazine that focuses on agriculture would be a waste of time and money for a collection agency that serves the medical industry. The following lists are online sources for submitting your press releases:

Fee-based press release submission engines:

- www.clickpress.com
- http://prweb.com
- www.prnewswire.com
- www.webwire.com

Free press release submission engines

- http://pressexposure.com
- www.przoom.com
- www.addpr.com/addrelease.php
- www.directionsmag.com/pressreleases/add
- www.free-press-release.com

Cold calls

An age-old concept for getting new business, especially when it comes to collection clients, is cold calling. The name itself gives the average person the chills because a dread of making phone calls to people and business representatives that you do not know conjures up the fear of the unknown. For one, cold calling a possible client might make you feel as if you are

disturbing the other party. When you think about it, though, all marketing and promotions are about getting someone's attention who might have an interest in what you are selling, which, in this case, is collection services.

The art of cold calling is not to start selling your services immediately to the person on the other end of the line. On the contrary, the initial call should be to test the lead and find the person you should be speaking with if the company has debt accounts that need collection services. In reality, the initial call is an information-seeking call in which you are trying to determine if the company is a hot lead, mediocre lead, or a cold lead (not worth pursuing).

The best questions to ask during the initial phone call include:

- Does your company ever have problem clients that do not pay on time or at all?
- Does your company currently use collection services?
- What are some of the issues you have with your current collection agency?
- What are the most important strengths of your current collection agency?
- Would it be possible for me to send you some information in the mail or via email?

Ask your contacts if you can send them some information. If they have some interest in debt collection services, they will agree to receive the literature. Give the contacts a week or two to review your information and then follow up with a phone call. Ask the prospects if they received the information, and from this point, you might want to ask if you can meet with them to go over what you have to offer and how it might benefit their companies. If you are lucky, the prospects will agree to a meeting. When you attend the meeting, be prepared and bring pertinent literature. The ideal is for the prospects to agree to a proposal. If the company is located out of state or too far away for a face-to-face meeting, schedule a conference call or a webinar where you can give your presentation online and while talking by phone.

Getting Your Business Online

Having an online presence in global commerce is essential. This broadens the span of clients that you will be able to pursue. Prospects from around the world will have access to you by logging on and querying collection agencies. Steps to getting online have to be considered before running out, buying a domain name, and throwing up a website to represent your business. Web-hosting firms are in no way scarce, so there are a few things to look for in a web-hosting provider, including:

- **Tech support reliability**

    o   Ask colleagues about potential selections, and check references to find out if a web-hosting firm responds to and corrects technical problems within an acceptable amount of time.

- **Web-hosting packages: email size and quantity**

    o   There are many packages from which to choose. Do not make the mistake of choosing a package based solely on the fact that it offers the lowest monthly rate. Find out what is included within each package. Most firms offer at least three hosting packages, if not more; so, you can choose a package that includes the features you need and costs the amount of money you have to spend.

- **Search engine optimization (SEO)**

    o   Search engines do not find your website automatically when it is created. A quality web-hosting firm must have the capability to help you submit your site to popular search engines such as Yahoo, Google, and Bing™.

- **Website design capabilities**

  o   Some firms offer ready-made templates. This is fine in some respects, but as your company grows, seek out a firm that can provide you with unique, interactive, and creative Web design capabilities.

Once you have found a hosting firm that meets your criteria, select a domain name that is easy to remember and relates to your industry. For example, www.abccollectionagency.com denotes exactly the type of services the company offers and is quite memorable.

Getting online does not ensure your name is at the top of the list when collection agency queries are executed. This is where search engine optimization (SEO) comes into place. SEO is the art of designing and integrating website graphics and writing marketing copy to increase top-level ranking from search queries. If your selected firm does not include copywriting services, you can always hire a freelance writer with SEO expertise to help you craft the right words for your website.

Using social media and networking

Social networking is proving to be one of the most effective forms of marketing a business online. Social network marketing is the Internet version of word-of-mouth advertising. Social networks, essentially, are online communities in which people connect with and share information with one another. Although the actual format will vary from one network to another, most social networks allow members to upload blog posts, send email or communication messages, upload pictures, instant message, join forums, and more. The main objective is to allow members who have the same interests to interact and exchange information.

Social media connect people across the world from the privacy of their own homes or office, with free access and instant gratification or access. Some social networking sites are more focused on personal interactions, but several focus their efforts on business networking. Still yet, some social media sites allow for some combination of both.

Many small businesses are finding social networking to be a great way to build and grow, especially in tough economic times when advertising budgets have been cut. Instead of paying for costly advertising, you are spreading information through word-of-mouth and websites that are generally free to use.

How it works

Social networking sites tend to have millions of members. These sites create an excellent opportunity for an individual to expand and promote a business without having to pay for advertising. With social networking, you can build an image and develop your customer base. To increase website traffic, many site owners are quickly realizing the value social networking sites have in drawing new customers. The following are some ideas on how to use social networking sites to generate website traffic:

- Completely fill out your social media profile with information about your business that includes a link from your profile to your website.

- On your business website, complete the loop by including a link from your website to each of your social media profiles.

- Use social bookmarking to increase your website's exposure on social networking sites. Social bookmarking sites include StumbleUpon (**www.stumbleupon.com**), Digg˜ (**http://digg.com**), and Reddit (**www.reddit.com**). Social bookmarking sites allow you to mark your favorite websites online so you can share them with others who might have an interest in the site. When someone has an interest in your collection agency, they can bookmark your site and then share this with their colleagues. It is a way of providing exposure to your business on the Internet.

- Create and share photos and videos on Flickr˚ (**www.flickr.com**) and YouTube (**www.youtube.com**) describing your business, products, and services. You also can upload these pictures and videos to your other social networking sites, such as Facebook (**www.facebook. com**), LinkedIn˚ (**www.linkedin.com**), and Twitter (**www.twitter. com**), to name but a few.

- Use social-networking forums to promote your business, website, and blog by sharing useful and relevant information or posing insightful questions for others in your industry or related businesses to answer for you. Promote your business through your social networking profiles, with links to your home page, but also by sharing special deals or promotions you are running for your collection service from time to time.

Popular social networking sites

A variety of social networking sites are available, and there might even be ones specific to your niche or specialization. Use the following site descriptions to find out which ones are best for your business and professional use:

Orkut is a popular social networking site owned by Google. This social networking site has millions of users; 59 percent of Orkut traffic originates from Brazil, followed by India with 30.4 percent. Like other sites, such as

Facebook, Orkut permits the creation of groups known as "communities" based on a designated subject and allows other people to join the communities. Orkut is an online community that can be used to engage potential clients and employees. If your business is located in one of these countries or services one of these countries, Orkut could be beneficial for your business presence.

Facebook is the leading social networking site, with more than 750 million active users at the time of publication. Initially, Facebook was developed to connect university students, but over time, the site became available publicly and its popularity exploded. You can now find Facebook users that range from high school students to retirees and grandparents, and all age groups and lifestyles in between. Facebook offers built-in tools and applications that make it easy for businesses to reach their target audiences or for individuals to interact with one another.

Myspace is a social networking website that offers an interactive platform for all its users. It allows the sharing of files, pictures, and even music videos. You can view the profiles of colleagues, competitors, potential clients, and any other users; you also can create and share blogs. Users often compare Facebook to Myspace, but one major difference between the two websites is the level of customization. Myspace is a large social networking site that allows users to decorate their profiles using HTML and CSS, while Facebook only allows plain text. The most prominent feature that makes Myspace unique among other sites is its affiliate program. If the affiliate product you are selling has a broad appeal, you might want consider using Myspace to market your collection agency, as you will be able to reach the largest crowd quickly.

YouTube is another social networking site owned by Google. To become a member of YouTube, go to the "Create Account" page, choose a username and password, enter your information, and click the "I Agree" button. YouTube is the largest video-sharing network site in the world, and it is a great place to do video marketing. For a collection agency, you might record videos on topics such as "How to identify when your collection accounts are dragging your business down" or "What to look for in a collection agency."

Digg (http://digg.com) is a place to discover and share content from around the Web, from the smallest blog to major news outlets. Digg is unique compared to other social networking sites because it allows you to network directly with people and directly sell to them. Once a post is submitted, it appears on a list in the selected category. From there, it will either fall in ranking or rise in ranking, depending on how people vote. Digg is actually what is known as a "social bookmarking" site. You submit your content to Digg, and other Digg users — known as Diggers — will review and rate it. Once it is rated high enough, your content could get posted on the home page of Digg, which gets thousands of visitors a day, potentially driving tons of traffic to your website or blog. Digg also allows you to locate articles online about your business, yourself, or something of interest to potential customers and then post them on them on the site. You also can find articles of interest others have put up on the site for readers to rate. You should even "Digg" all of the articles or blog posts you write and post online yourself. SEO experts suggest you also Digg each of the pages on your website.

Twitter is different from other social networking sites, and the popularity of Twitter has grown at an amazing rate. With Twitter, you can provide followers with updates on new services your agency offers from your phone or computer. When you sign up with Twitter, you can use the service to post and receive messages (known as a "tweet") with your Twitter account, and the service distributes it to your followers. In turn, you receive all the messages sent from those you wish to follow. Twitter is a text-based social network in which you only have 140 characters to send out an update, or a tweet, to let your followers know what you have to say.

Flickr is a photo and video sharing website that lets you organize and store your photos online. You can upload from your desktop, send by email, or use your camera phone. It has features to get rid of red eye, crop a photo, or get creative with fonts and effects. Google Picasa™ is another great photo sharing and storing application.

Popular business networking sites

The following sites offer networking opportunities specifically for business owners:

- **BizFriendz (www.bizfriendz.com)**: Make new contacts, promote your products and services, get viral exposure to your business, and earn commissions while you build your network. The site is made up of business people and business owners who are the decision-makers you should connect with to help land their collection account business.

- **Biznik˚ (www.biznik.com)**: Their tagline is "Business networking that doesn't suck." This site is geared directly to entrepreneurs and business owners, with a number of different communities. Again, because this is a community in which business owners and entrepreneurs are lingering, this is the audience you need to connect with to help them collect on their past due accounts.

- **Cofoundr (www.cofoundr.com)**: A private community for entrepreneurs that promises to help members build teams and network with other entrepreneurs. Entrepreneurs typically own one or more business entity. They also tend to run in circles with other business owners and entrepreneurs, so these are the people you need to be connecting with for your particular industry.

- **Ecademy (www.ecademy.com)**: Provides extra tools to build your business, such as networking events, webinars on online topics, and the ability to locate members with specific knowledge

- **Fast Pitch (www.fastpitchnetworking.com)**: Reports it is growing faster than any other social network for professionals. Set up your own profile page and network with other business people.

- **Konnects˚ (www.konnects.com)**: Gives each member a profile page. Join communities, to meet other members, and network with professionals with similar interests or that are potential clients for your business.

- **LinkedIn (www.linkedin.com)**: Connect and network with others in your field or who can use your abilities and/or services.

- **StartupNation˚ (www.startupnation.com)**: Active forums with a wide variety of subjects for businesses. This site might not benefit you as much for a collection business, but it could provide you with contacts, resources, and information on running a business in general.

- **StumbleUpon (www.stumbleupon.com)**: Post any information of value and interest to others that pertains to your business or industry. Similar to Digg, this is a social bookmarking site or news-sharing site.

- **Upspring˜ (www.upspring.com)**: Increase exposure and attract more customers. Sign up free and get a profile page, find and join groups, and increase your networking activities.

- **XING (www.xing.com)**: An active group of professionals looking for ways to network with people of interest. This might include fellow collection agency owners who you can learn from or finding businesses that might have a need for one or more of your collection services.

Blogging to success

Once a business is online, a great tool to add to your website is a blog. A blog is a form of social networking in which you can share tips, advice, articles, and information. Blogs allow publishers to write about issues that affect their industries, upcoming events, articles, and whatever is pertinent or important to readers.  Your blog also can be used to inform your clients of new services or changes in services. You might choose to have one employee in charge of maintaining the blog or allow various employees in your organization to contribute. You can even employ experts as guest bloggers to share information with your readers that pertain to them but that might fall outside of your own expertise. Blogging does require a sense of commitment and consistency, so, if you cannot add new blog posts at least two or three times per week, it is not an effective marketing tool for your business.

If you do start a blog, however, make sure the overall topics on your blog all relate somehow to the collection business. In other words, you want to create a niche blog your current and potential customers come to for your expertise and the industry news you share on a topic of interest to them. In this case, the topic relates to debt collection, but from the business owners' points of view. Each blog post can and should cover different aspects of debt collection. Some examples include ways to collect on delinquent accounts, the ins and outs of credit reporting, tips for reducing your collection account debts (for businesses). Postings do not have to be lengthy, and the option to allow your readers to comment on your posts is strictly up to you. If you do decide to allow comments, pay particular attention to what is being posted on your blog.

Other Ways to Network and Find Clients

As the saying goes, "It is all in who you know," and that is especially important when opening a new business. Becoming involved in local associations or organizations can bring attention to your agency as affiliating yourself and your business with professionals might enable you to become business partners or even acquire potential clients.

Chambers of Commerce

Chambers of Commerce organizations have a wealth of information on local business communities and offer resources to help run and grow a viable business. It is to their benefit that companies succeed, as it leads to a prosperous community overall. The chambers tend to put on many events that require professionals to host and attend, which are great opportunities for business owners to showcase their public speaking prowess and create recognition for a business.

Collection associations

Associations put businesses on the pulse of what is going on in the specific industry. With or without paying membership fees, associations can provide you with a wealth of information, providing tools, articles, events, and resources to help operate your business.

Some examples of associations geared toward collection professionals include:

- The Association of Credit and Collection International (**www.acainternational.org**)
- Commercial Collection Agency Association (**www.ccascollect.com**)

- NACARA — North American Collection Agency Regulatory Association (**www.nacara.info**)
- Debt Collection Agency (**www.caine-weiner.com/about/association-memberships.php**)

Referrals

If you run a good business and help others succeed, you can expect to have many client referrals sent your way. There is no other lead like a referral because the prospect already has a good feeling about and background information on the business he or she is being referred to.

Although referrals might come your way because your satisfied clients want to pass your information on to other business owners who need your help, you also can go after referral business proactively. For example, after working with a client for six months or a year, send out a referral request letter or email to these clients. In other words, ask them if they know of any other businesses that can benefit from your services, just as they have. You can decide whether you want to offer an incentive or small reward gift for any referrals that might then become clients.

Using Proposals to Close the Sale

Once there is a qualified lead with a potential client, the next step is to have an in-depth conversation or meeting with the client so you can better assess his or her needs. Once you have a better idea of what the needs of the business are, you can develop a proposal personalized and customized to those needs. Use your presentation to illustrate the collection problems the client is having and how your business can resolve these problems.

Proposal formats and presentation can vary from company to company, and even slightly from representative to representative. What works for one set of clients might not appeal to other types of clients. Overall, however, you do want your proposals to maintain the brand image of your collection business that you have worked so hard to create throughout all of your marketing planning and work.

Some of the items a formal proposal for a client might include are:

- Letter of introduction to the business
- List and description of services your business offers
- Cost associated with each of the services or package deal prices
- Payment options

All of the material included in the proposal should be printed on your company letterhead, should be assembled in a professional portfolio or folder, and should include one or two of your business cards. Once the proposal has been submitted, put it on your calendar to follow up with the prospect within three to five business days. In fact, indicate in your introduction letter the date you will reach out to them to answer any questions they may have. At the very least, you can follow up to confirm their receipt of the information and then schedule an appointment to talk or meet to discuss the information further.

Using the Better Business Bureau as a Business Benefit

You are probably familiar with the Better Business Bureau® (BBB®) as a consumer protection agency against unethical business practices. The BBB, however, is also a national, private agency that businesses can use to their advantage as well. Because collection agencies tend to have a bad reputation, being a member of the BBB adds credibility to your business. Primarily, the BBB helps reputable businesses maintain a positive and productive reputation with the public by offering accreditation. Obtaining accreditation from the BBB signifies that your agency has made a commitment to executing sound business practices such as resolving any consumer complaints.

When customers see that your agency is accredited by the BBB, it is confirmation of your commitment to run a legitimate business that provides quality services and a high level of customer satisfaction. The BBB is recognized throughout the United States and Canada. Alignment with the BBB, your website, and referrals allow potential clients to find out information easily about your company's background and make a decision to select your agency over another.

Rules for accreditation:

- Building trust
- Adhering to established standards for advertising and selling
- Exhibiting honest representation of products and services and providing clear disclosure of all material terms
- Being transparent with the vital details of business foundations such as the nature, location, and ownership
- Properly disclosing policies, guarantees, and procedures that affect a customer's decision to use your services

On the other end of the spectrum, for instance, an agency that does not abide by the standards of quality and service set by the BBB also can be a warning to prospective clients. The BBB does not maliciously attack any business but rather acts as an investigative liaison between those making a complaint and the parties responsible for running the business. The BBB provides a rating for a business based upon the information provided by external sources, including customer complaints, government actions, and advertising issues. Based on multiple criteria, the BBB grades a company from A to F with pluses and minuses, with A-pluses being the highest grade, just like in school.

There are circumstances in which a company would receive a grade of NR (no rating), which makes the company ineligible to be graded. There are multiple reasons for this, including if the business is no longer in operation or if the business is in bankruptcy.

The organization makes it very clear on its website (**www.bbb.org**) that its rating reflects its opinion based upon information it has received and the organization's experience, so the rating is not a complete guarantee of a business' reliability or performance.

Eligibility to join the BBB

Unfortunately, not every business is eligible for accreditation. If a business does not meet the criteria set by the organization, the business will not be permitted to join or receive accreditation. Any business interested in becoming accredited can apply. If your agency is approved for accreditation, fees are associated with receiving and maintaining the accreditation. For more information on how to become accredited, contact your local BBB office and speak with a representative.

Summary

Regardless of how you choose to go about it, the purpose of advertising and promoting your business is to get potential clients. At first, it might work to target small, medium, or large businesses or possibly select companies according to the industry or region. Whichever choice is selected, the key is to focus on that particular market so you can focus your marketing efforts on the best ways to reach these markets. As things change in your business or if the particular target market shows it is not profitable, changes can be made to accommodate this.

Chapter 10

Agency Proposals — What to Include and How to Present Them

The ultimate goal of any business that hires your agency to collect on its debts is to recover the most money possible. You might be the firm that fits the needs of the company perfectly, but you first have to be able to convince the company decision-maker that this is the case. The way you do this is to create and deliver a proposal to the client. Although you might have a template for your proposal, you always will have to customize and modify the proposal to address the specific concerns of the client you will be meeting. Although you always want to put your best foot forward, you have to learn how to listen, identify the hot buttons for the prospect, and then find ways to weave solutions to these hot buttons into your presentation.

Before you even can start to assemble a proposal or presentation materials for the client, however, you first have to act somewhat like an investigator to uncover the information you need to put together an educated and well-informed proposal.

Prepare to Discuss Your Proposal

Before you type the first word on the proposal, schedule an in-depth phone or face-to-face meeting with the decision maker of the company. Depending on how some companies are structured, you might even need to meet with several different people in the organization. Each person you meet with or talk to will provide the insight you need to identify what it is important to the client.

Some companies might have accepted that with the set of accounts they want you to work on, they never will receive the full amount due to them from every debtor. This means that there is a percentage or certain recovery amount acceptable to them. The recovery amount is the amount the debt collector able is able to obtain from the debtor, even if it is less than the full debt owed. Through your conversations, the company representatives might not come right out and give you the fact or figure, but through deductive reasoning you might be able to determine a range. You can hone in on this range and then include it as one of the points in your presentation.

When a client hires you, and you are going through the process of working out your agreement, the client will tell you how much leeway you have to negotiate with debtors. Before you start working on the accounts, the negotiation range is information that you already would have discussed with the client. The client will tell you how much he or she is willing to give in to debtors before you ever get on the phone with the debtor.

For example, a debtor might owe $5,000. He might say it is too much for him to pay but might ask what deals your company can offer if he agrees to pay a lump sum payment at that moment. You might say that you can only negotiate it down to $4,000, but know that your client is willing to accept as low as 50 percent of the debt. The debtor might then say that $4,000 is still too much for him, but he could maybe come up with about $3,000. Because this falls within the parameters of what you know your client will accept, you can agree to accept the $3,000 payment from the debtor. Thus, the debtor feels he is free from debt, and the client got a satisfactory amount of the money they were due.

Keep in mind that the proposal is your way of painting the best picture possible so you can win their business. In the same respect, you also have to be realistic about what you promise the client you can and cannot do for them.

What to include in a proposal

After your discussions with the representatives of the company, you should have gathered enough information to start assembling the proposal. As stated earlier, many of the items you include in the proposal are template; you only need to modify or fill in the details. Other pieces that go into the proposal are created once and get included in every proposal to every prospective client.

Some of the items you should include in a proposal:

- Introduction letter
- Testimonials
- Collection agreement
- Basic company information
- Services
- Collection service agreement
- Costs and payment options
- Services
    o Collection letters
    o Phone calls
    o NSF
    o Legal
    o Any additional services

Whether you are presenting the proposal in person, sending it via email, or regular mail might also affect the pieces you include in the proposal. For example, if you are presenting the proposal in person, you might not have to include the collection agreement in the packet you hand over to the client during your meeting. You could work to close the sale, and as a way of doing so, you would then pull out the collection agreement to discuss and have the client sign at that time.

Sample proposal package

Introduction letter

June 01, 2014

Prospective client name
Prospective client phone and address

Dear Prospective Client:

We appreciate the opportunity to provide you with this proposal to [insert description of the services you discussed with the client]. We have reviewed your current needs and feel confident that our agency is fully qualified to work on collecting the money due to you on your outstanding accounts. We understand that these outstanding account balances have a dramatic affect on your cash flow and the overall profitability of your business.

ABC Collection Agency has been in business for five years. During our five years in business, we have developed a stellar record for aggressively recovering funds while maintaining a good reputation in the community. We have a satisfied client base that would be more than willing to vouch for our standards.

After going over this proposal, we will be more than happy to discuss any questions you might have. Please feel free to contact us at (800) 000-0000. We look forward to doing business with you.

Sincerely,

John Doe
President

Basic company information

ABC Collection Agency
1 Collection Drive, Suite 5D, Recovery City, FL 32839
(800) 000-0000
www.ABCCollectionAgency.com
Years in business: 10
Status: Privately Held
CEO: John Doe (email: jdoe@abccollectionagency.com)

ABC Collection Agency was founded by CEO John Doe after working as a credit manager for a Fortune 500 company. Doe successfully ensured the Fortune 500 business maintained streamlined processes for extending credit. He also oversaw the accounts receivables and collection department. Within this position, Doe received several awards for his work.

In 2004, Doe began ABC Collection Agency with one collection representative and one office manager. Today, ABC Collection Agency has expanded to employ 15 employees, including nine trained collection representatives, and we service more than 150 clients spread throughout the United States.

We are an equal opportunity agency and will not discriminate against a prospective client, account, or employee based on lawful practices.

Testimonials

Do not take our word for it. Our clients are satisfied with our services, continue to place accounts with us, and expand to use our other services, such as accounts receivable outsourcing.

"I cannot believe how fast ABC Collection Agency recovered an eight-month-old debt with a balance of $8,000. We tried everything, even other collection agencies, to try to collect our money. I definitely would recommend ABC Collection Agency to any company with large and old debt sitting on their books."

—Aaron Temple, Credit Manager

"I appreciated the fact that ABC Collection Agency provided us with new account updates immediately without our having to call them repeatedly to see what they were doing."

—Jeffrey Daniels, President

"Since we have outsourced our accounts receivables with ABC Collection Agency, it has freed up the accounting department, allowing us to execute due diligence on other issues. And our receivables have never been so current."

—Mike Bledsoe, CFO

"We have been working with ABC Collection Agency since they opened their doors, right next door to us, and we could not be more satisfied."

—Steve Burroughs, CEO

Complete list of services

Collection	Letters
Legal action	Skip tracing
Accounts receivable outsourcing	NSF check collection
Credit reporting	Credit counseling

Proposal detail

ABC Collection Agency is providing ____[client]____ with this proposal based upon the needs and interest expressed by the client. The pricing and services included reflects this as well. Any additional services needed by__[client]__ can be added as needed by [added to the contract by amendment to the original contact], and ABC Collection Agency will provide_[client's name]_ with associated fees within a reasonable amount of time.

ABC Collection Agency is a full-service agency that adheres to the laws governing the industry and will aggressive pursue account while not defying these laws. __[Client's name]__ agrees to not request or imply that any unjust collection practice be pursued that may violate these laws.

Requested Services:

- Collection
  - o ABC Collection Agency will pursue collection on your accounts with 72 hours of submission. This also includes necessary steps needed to skip trace a client or asset to begin recovering your funds. First collection will be sent to the address provided, and with 30 days, ABC Collection Agency will pursue phone call collection. ABC Collection Company will document all important information on the account and provide a biweekly update report unless 75 percent or full payment has been made.

- Skip tracing
  - o ABC Collection Agency will provide skip-tracing services on those accounts of which they have received returned collection letters or have not make successful phone communication. ABC Collection Agency agrees to pursue in-house skip tracing. If it is recommended that outside skip-tracing services will be required, we will notify in advance before charging additional fees.

- Credit Reporting
  - o ABC Collection Agency will report to credit bureaus all excessively delinquent accounts on the behalf of _[client's name]_.

Fees: Enter your fees based on how your agency charges for services.

Payment Options: As a client of ABC Collection Agency, you have the option of making your payment via credit card, bank card, or check. *Depending on how you negotiate with your client, you might be able to subtract the percentage owed to your agency from the payment received from the debtor.*

Proposals never should be generic; rather, they should be catered to the specific needs expressed by the client. The additional information included in the proposal, such as the services list, clearly will let the prospect know about the other services you have to offer.

Getting the Proposal Signed

During the presentation or discussion, the goal is not to reiterate all information in the proposal, but rather to highlight key points that meet the prospect's specific needs. Most importantly, be prepared to answer any questions the client might have. You do not need to read over the entire proposal package with the client if you already have had previous discussions that cover the same information.

Most upfront work goes into enticing a prospect to become a new client, so when a client finally agrees to do business with your agency, you might get so excited that you want to accept the business on the client's word and a handshake. For the most part, clients are honest and possess integrity. However, in the professional world of business, coming to an agreement involves much more than the client's word and a handshake on the deal, so you need to move from the proposal agreement to a formally signed agreement or contract to employ your services. Use a legal agreement, preferably drawn up by or at least reviewed by a

lawyer, that the client must sign and return to you before you formally begin working on collecting for the business.

Collection service agreement

The collection agreement is the glue that holds the proposal together. This legal document clearly defines the responsibilities of both the agency and the client. Because this is the legally binding document, the deal is not complete, or is not really a deal, until the agreement is signed. One of the key factors a good collection agreement includes is a stipulation that your agency is the only collection agency working on the accounts you have agreed to handle for the company. In other words, you do not want to be competing against another collection agency trying to collect on the same accounts. Many services agreements include a clause to hold the agency harmless against certain legal claims. Collection agreements also will include appropriate fees to be charged to the client. Writing collection agreements are not for novices; only an attorney can draw up such a complex, binding, legal document, so include this as part of your budget when you are forming your business and before taking on clients.

An example excerpt from a collection agreement is below:

FEES AND OTHER PROVISIONS

CONTINGENCY FEE — Client agrees to pay ABC Collection Agency for its collection efforts based on the fee schedule (below) that applies to all funds collected. No fees are charged on uncollected balances, not including withdrawal fees (see below).

Fifteen (15) percent of amounts collected on accounts less than eight (8) months from date of last charge or payment. (Excluding finance charges and/or collection fees)

Twenty-five (25) percent of amounts collected on accounts older than eight (8) months (Excluding finance charges and/or collection fees)

Forty-five (45) percent of amounts collected on accounts previously handled by another agency or forwarded to other agencies.

Summary

In the age of technology, a lot of business is being done online and via email. However, when submitting proposals, you might want to remove technology from the equation. Although technology can be convenient, many mishaps can occur when using email and electronic documents. If a prospect does not receive the emailed proposal or cannot open the attached documents, it can delay the process, and time tends to kill deals. Hand delivered or professionally delivered proposals — via FedEx, UPS, USPS, or a courier — ensure delivery and even provide a more professional appearance. On the other hand, when time is of the essence or the client prefers electronic handling of the documents, you have the option to acquiesce to their request.

Once you have supplied the prospect with your proposal, try to contact them within the next 24 to 48 hours to go over the details or answer any questions they might have. Never let your proposal go stale; continue to follow up with the prospect until you find out if they will use your services or have decided to go with another agency.

Chapter 11

Laws and Regulations Governing the Industry

Protecting consumer privacy has always been an important factor of doing business. However, with millions of Americans in debt, the average American household has more than $10,000 in credit card debt. On top of the credit card debt they are carrying, consumers also are carrying other debt, such as student loans, car loans, and medical bills. Although many consumers are able to keep up with paying at least the minimum payment due on each of their bills, other consumers fall behind. To make the matter worse, the recession that began in 2007 increased the unemployment rate to record high levels, the housing and lending market practically collapsed, and more Americans found themselves in financial situations where they could not even afford to buy essentials such as food and medicine, let alone make a payment on their credit card.

This situation provides a big boost to the collection business. Original creditors, also hurting from the downturn in the economy, began contacting more of their customers in an attempt to get their own financial situations straight. The situation also led more businesses that could not collect these debts on their own to professional collection agencies to do it for them.

Though debtors certainly can make it difficult for businesses and even a collection agency to collect on the debt, the government has strict policies governing the protection of the privacy of these debtors and even how a collection agency goes about collecting on the debt. For example, the Federal Trade Commission (FTC) is an arm of the government that protects consumer interests and commerce by preventing unfair competition.

Beyond privacy, the government has enacted several laws to protect consumers from unfair collection practices. One of the primary laws is the Fair Debt Collection Practices Act (FDCPA). This Federal law does not cover commercial collection services, which means it does not cover businesses or organizations that collection agencies are trying to collect from. The consumer protection covers consumers, households, and personal debt, as well as third-party debt collection.

Under the FDCPA, there are practices collection agencies are prohibited from using to collect from a debtor. Some of these practices include:

1. **Harassment of the debtor** — Debt collectors may not harass, oppress, or abuse debtors or any third parties they contact. For example, they may not:

   • Use threats of violence or harm against the debtor
   • Use obscene language toward a debtor
   • Use the phone to annoy a debtor

2. **Make false statements** — Debt collectors may not lie when they are trying to collect a debt. For example, they may not:

   • Falsely claim the debtor has committed a crime

- Falsely represent that the collection agency operates or works for a credit reporting company if they do not
- Misrepresent the amount the debtor owes

3. **Debt collectors are prohibited from saying the following:**

- The debtor will be arrested if he or she does not pay the debt.
- The collector will seize or sell the debtor's property or wages unless he or she pays the amount of debt owed.
- Legal action will be taken against the debtor.

Make sure you understand what you are restricted from saying to debtors so you can teach any collection representatives working for you what they are restricted from saying to debtors as well. You might find yourself or your business in legal trouble of your own. For more information on FDCPA, visit **www.ftc.gov/bcp/edu/pubs/consumer/credit/cre18.shtm**.

Other Federal Credit Laws Affecting Collection

Sometimes debtors do not pay their bills because they are not satisfied with the service, feel that they were taken advantage of, or the creditor has broken the law or committed fraud. When a consumer brings up these issues, they must be addressed with the client. There will be times when the creditor was aware of the customer complaint or reason for not paying the bill. This is pertinent information that will affect how you work these accounts. If your client has broken any laws or statutes, you may not be able to collect the money from the debtor. Two of the primary laws to consider are the Truth in Lending Act and the Fair Credit Billing Act.

The Truth in Lending Act

The Truth in Lending Act states that businesses extending credit must provide an estimate of the total cost for items purchased or leased. In simple terms, a creditor should provide a clear picture of what the consumer is getting into financially. This law came into effect because companies that were extending credit or leases initially did not provide the total cost of the product or service in the long term, so consumers did not realize how much they were paying for the item after including the interest on top of the principal amount. By providing these costs up front, it helps consumers make better purchasing decisions. Lenders, banks, and financial institutions must disclose the following information:

- Payment due dates
- Monthly finance charges
- Annual interest rates
- Total price paid over time versus the price of an item if paid up front with cash
- Annual interest rate
- Late payments fees

The law's goal is to enable the consumer to compare credit or loan terms between lenders so that they can make an informed financial decision. The Truth in Lending Act also works to limit balloon payment mortgages, which is a mortgage in which borrowers pay principal and interest payments for a period, and then at the end of the period the full principal amount is due in full.

The act is associated with the Federal Deposit Insurance Corporation (FDIC) and can be cited as the Consumer Credit Protection Act. If your client's customer can prove the client has violated one or all of the laws within this act, not only will your client not be able to collect on the debt, but they can be fined up to $5,000, imprisoned up to one year, or both. If you are not able to collect on the debt on behalf of the client, you will not receive payment. Details on the law can be found at **www.fdic.gov/regulations/laws**. Because the court case would be between the client and the debtor, the court determines whether the debtor has sufficient evidence that the client violated the law. Some collection agencies do offer it as a service to represent their clients in court, but typically, the client hires an attorney to manage these legal issues.

The Fair Credit Billing Act

The Fair Credit Billing Act was put into place to help consumers resolve billing disputes of "open-end" credit accounts, such as credit cards. The FTC is the agency that ensures the billing practices for these types of accounts are fair to consumers and handles consumer disputes against companies. These unfair practices include:

- Unauthorized charges
- Charges that list the wrong date or amount
- Charges for goods and services the consumer did not accept or that were not delivered as agreed
- Calculation errors
- Failure to post payments and other credits, such as returns
- Failure to send bills to your current address — provided the creditor receives your change of address, in writing, at least 20 days before the billing period ends
- Charges for which the consumer asks for an explanation or written proof of purchase along with a claimed error or request for clarification

The debtor is required to initiate the process to dispute the issue with the biller by taking these steps:

- Write to the creditor at the address given for "billing inquiries," not the address for sending payments, and include their name, address, account number, and a description of the billing error.

- Send the letter so that it reaches the creditor within 60 days after the first bill containing the error was mailed to the debtor.

If the debtor that has been fraudulently charged and the creditor cannot or does not resolve the dispute, or the debtor has made an identity theft claim with the FTC, you as a collection professional and your client will not be able to report a delinquency to the customer's credit report until the FTC has issued a decision in the investigation of the dispute. *Chapter 13 discusses reporting delinquencies to the credit bureaus.*

Once a debtor successfully has initiated his or her complaint, the company (your client) receives notification of the complaint. The client must respond to the FTC and the debtor within 90 days of the complaint being filed to explain the validity of the bill or make the necessary corrections. If your client neglects to follow these procedures, they will forfeit the ability to collect the amount in dispute or any related finance charges up to $50. Note: This act does not cover disputes related to the quality of goods or services.

Other Billing Rights that May Affect a Client's Recovery of Funds

Businesses that offer "open-end" credit also must:

- Provide customers with written notification of the customer's right to dispute billing errors when the customer first opens the account and a few other times throughout the year.

- Send an account statement for each billing period as long as the customer owes more than one dollar.

- Have the bill statement to the customer at least 14 days before the due date.

- Apply payments to the customer's account on the date received.

- Credit or refund overpayments and other amounts owed to a customer. If the customer requests a refund check to be mailed, the check must be mailed within seven business days after the creditor receives the written request.

The Red Flags Rule

Identity theft is on the rise and is a crime that is becoming easier to commit. Millions of Americans have their identities stolen each year. With new technology and the Internet, information is much easier to spread around and get into the hands of the wrong people. Because of this, the FTC has instituted the **Red Flags Rule**, which requires businesses and organizations to set standards or warning signs to prevent identity theft before the crime is committed.

This means that if a debtor files a complaint saying that your client fraudulently sold products or services to someone who stole the debtor's identity, your client will not be able to require the victim of identity theft to pay.

The FTC provides guidelines businesses should put in writing as rules to identity fraud to make sure the company does not sell the products or services to a customer who is using someone else's identity. The FTC does require businesses to post their written policies and procedures, which are:

- There must be written reasonable program policies and procedures in place to identify red flags for identity theft in day-to-day operations. For example, if the average sale of your company is $500 and a customer orders $5,000 worth of product, your policy should require some additional verification that the person placing the order is in fact the credit card holder. The company might have the credit card company contact the credit card holder to verify the order is legitimate.

- Once identity theft has been identified, the client should report it to the FTC immediately.

- Because identity theft is an ever-changing threat, companies must address how it will re-evaluate the program periodically to reflect new risks from this crime.

Your client will have to check with the FTC to see if they must comply with the Red Flags Rule and proceed with plans of action. Once again, if down the road, you or your client realizes they have sold products or services to a customer fraudulently, they will have little recourse for making the unknowing debtor pay up. Many times, the thief is not identified, so the client typically has to write off the debt.

Using the Wrong Language: Threats and Abusive Verbiage

In 2007, a large Houston-based collection agency agreed to pay $1.375 million in damages to settle charges that the agency threatened consumers. The FDCPA firmly prohibits collection agencies from verbally abusing consumers. The FTC has found that abusive debt collection practices contribute to the number of bankruptcies, marital instability, loss of jobs, and invasion of privacy. A few things to consider when communicating with debtors include:

- In written documentation, do not use faux attorney letterhead to convince someone that they are receiving legal documentation. If the agency would like a letter sent to the debtor from an attorney, hire one.

- Replica and false documentation that looks like official documentation, such as replica legal documents, never should be used.

- A collection professional is prohibited from threatening a debtor with jail or prosecution. Collectors are not attorneys or judges and have no legal right to offer legal advice.

- If there is no legal action pending, do not send documentation to debtors using the terms "versus" or "plaintiff."

- Never threaten bodily or property harm when speaking with a debtor.

You have to know the fine line between appropriate, aggressive collection tactics and harassment. A good collection professional knows how to be polite but persistent and does not break the law by making an unreasonable number of calls to a debtor within a short period.

The Fair Credit Reporting Act

The Fair Credit Reporting Act (FCRA) is a federal law that protects a debtor's privacy and ensures that all information reported to the credit bureaus is accurate. The goal of the act is to ensure the information that appears in each of the three credit reports is accurate and fair, so that fair lending decisions can be made. As a collection agency owner, you should understand the details of this law because your processes are intertwined with the credit bureaus' responsibility to follow this act. To make sure you know where you stand with credit bureaus, do the following things:

- Ensure that you provide the credit bureau with accurate data about a debtor's credit history.

- Document and validate all information reported and quickly respond to the credit bureaus inquiries.

- When a consumer disputes any information on their report submitted by the agency, you must investigate swiftly and respond to the inquiry within 30 days.

- Understand each credit bureau's standard for reporting information on a consumer's report.

Under the FCRA, your customer is entitled to the following information about their debt:

- **The customer must be told of the debt against him or her.** Anyone who uses a credit report or another type of consumer report to deny an application for credit, insurance, or employment — or to take another adverse action against a debtor — must tell the debtor and must give the debtor the name, address and phone number of the agency that provided the information.

- **The customer has the right to know what is in their file.** The debtor may request and obtain all the information in the files of a consumer-reporting agency (your "file disclosure"). For example, if a borrower is denied credit, they can obtain a free credit report from each of the three credit reporting agencies to see what negative information may have prohibited them from receiving the loan.

For more information regarding the laws that protect the consumer, please visit **www.ftc.gov/credit**. Become familiar with this information — it will come in handy in the future.

Summary

These are a few of the laws that require lenders, banks, and financial institutions to report and use accurate and fair information to make lending decisions. These laws also protect consumers to ensure fair treatment for lending and for billing practices. Although your role is to collect on bad debt, you should be aware of the laws you, consumers, lenders, and credit companies have to abide by in extending credit and then collecting on bad debt.

Chapter 12

Collection Methods and Communication

There is an order to the collection process. First, you must send the collection letter to inform the debtor that the creditor has sent the debt to collection. At this point, the debtor will respond, deny, or prepare for collection calls. Not sending the letter in advance causes additional work for the collection agency because the debtor may stall for time and request written documentation of the debt, which the debtor has the right to do according to the FDCPA.

First the Letter, Then the Call

Collection letters play a big role in the collection recovery process. The collection letters allow you to provide extensive detail on the bad debt and give a persuasive argument to move the reader to action.

As with all other activities, collection letters must follow guidelines set forth by the FDCPA. One rule is to include the **mini Miranda**. This Miranda informs the recipients of the letter whom they are dealing with and gives them the opportunity to decide how much information they choose to disclose. Furthermore, the Miranda informs the proposed debtor of their right to dispute a debt within 30 days.

Sample mini Miranda

This is an attempt to collect a debt; any information obtained will be used for that purpose. This communication is from a debt collector.

Unless you notify this office within 30 days after receiving this notice that you dispute the validity of this debt or any portion thereof, this office will assume this debt is valid. If you notify this office in writing within 30 days from receiving this notice that you dispute the validity of this debt or any portion thereof, this office will obtain verification of the debt or obtain a copy of a judgment and mail you a copy of such verification or judgment. If you request this office in writing within 30 days after receiving this notice, this office will provide you with the name and address of the original creditor, if different than the current creditor.

The mini Miranda serves a great purpose to the debtor: it notifies them that the debt collectors' goal is to do everything in their power to collect on an outstanding debt, and it tells the debtor that any information he or she provides can be used for debt collection purposes. This information includes address, phone number, employment information, bank account number, and any other information you can use legally to bring you closer to closing an outstanding account. Stay in control of the situation on your end, and obtain information that you may need to continue to pursue the debtor, such as getting permission to garnish their wages or bank account, which is when you directly debit a bank account for the amount of the debt payment. *Chapter 15 will explain garnishing in more detail.*

Keep letters professional

Keep in mind that collection letters must be written in a professional manner. It is okay to persuade a debtor to pay all or a portion of the debt, but emotionally charged language should not be included. For example, "Pay your bills!" or "Don't be a deadbeat!" can be misconstrued as harassment, and because it is written, it will be easier to prove in court.

A sample letter, on your collection agency letterhead, may read as such:

9.1.14

Jane Jones
12345 ABC St.
Anytown, USA 11111

RE: Account Number: 12345
        Amount Due: $2,897.15
        Claimant: XYZ Widget Co.

The payment records of our client XYZ Widget Co. indicate that the above referenced account is over 90 days past. The past due amount is $2,897.15 and is due immediately.

If you have already sent payment, you may disregard this notice.

If you wish to make payment arrangements, please contact our office immediately by phone, email, fax, or regular mail.

PLEASE NOTE: If you do not notify this office in writing within 30 days of this notice to dispute the validity of this debt, then it is considered a valid debt. If you do dispute the validity of this debt in writing within 30 days of receiving this notice, then we will obtain proof of the debt from our client or a copy of the judgment filed against you in court and provide you with a copy of this proof. Upon your request, we can also provide with you with the contact information of the original creditor, for which we are now collecting the debt. This letter is an attempt to collect on this debt and any information we obtain will be used for the purpose of collecting the debt.

Again, if you prefer to make payment arrangements, please contact our office.

Sincerely,

Katie D. Collector

Next Step: The Call

The letter is a good first step to establish the debt and verify the debtor's address. However, debtors can avoid your collection letters by saying they

never received the letter or that the letter was lost in the mail even if they chose not to open and instead throw it in the trash. Your next step is to try to get your debtor on the phone. Thirty days after sending out the collection letter, you will have to call the debtor to recover your client's funds.

Next to face-to-face communication, a phone call is the most effective way to persuade someone to pay on an outstanding bill. In fact, in the collection business, the phone is your primary tool for communicating

with debtors. It is rare, if not unheard of, for a collection representative to meet with debtors face-to-face in an effort to collect on a debt.

There is a strategy to make collection calls legally and successfully. FDCPA states that collection representatives must contact consumers during normal business hours, which it defines as 8 a.m. to 9 p.m. However, if the debtor requests to be contacted at a time that is more convenient for him or her, the collection agency must honor the request. Not honoring the request and continuing to call during normal business hours may be seen as harassment and would allow the debtor to file a complaint.

Defining whom you can talk to

According to the FDCPA, discussed in detail in Chapter 11, a collection company may not discuss personal information about a debtor with a third party. This includes employers, girlfriends, boyfriends, friends, relatives, or any third-party representative. A few exclusions include:

- The debtor's spouse
- The debtor's attorney
- Someone the debtor has given you permission to communicate with
- A consumer reporting agency

There are times when a debtor gives a collection company permission to communicate with a third party, such as an attorney or a financial planner. For example, if a debtor has an attorney, they may want you to work directly with the attorney to work out the debt. To protect the integrity of your company, it is a good idea to confirm this in writing via a letter sent by mail, facsimile, or email.

Using Notes to Validate Debtor Responsibilities

All accounting and collection software comes with the ability to make notes on accounts. As soon as you receive a debtor file from the client, you should add in everything you know about the debtor into your notes. The information you have can vary drastically from client to client. For example, you only may have a first and last name, last known address, and the balance the debtor owes your client. For another file, you may have all of this information, as well as copies of the collection letters and correspondence, and notes from phone calls made by the client to the debtor. The latter of the two files provides much more background information to you, so you have more information to work with before starting your own collection efforts.

Before picking up the phone, have the debtor's account open to the notes section. Review the notes that are currently in the system and make notes while talking on the phone. The next time you have a conversation with the debtor, you will sound more professional and help the debtor to overcome "debtor amnesia" about what your previous conversation entailed. The notes help you exude confidence when speaking with the debtor. If the debtor senses any form of uneasiness or lack of confidence, he or she may challenge the bill.

Managing outcome before the call

Now that you have everything in front of you to make the call, you have to prepare for the desired outcome. If there were previous communications with the debtor, there should be knowledge of their financial situation and personality. Have a goal for a minimum payment if it is not likely that full payment will be made. Schedule a payment plan in advance to prevent stalling while on the phone. However, if the planned due date needs to be altered to fit the debtor's payment schedule, do so. Always try to receive some form of payment, no matter if it is $1 on each call regardless of the debtor's situation. By law, it shows good faith on the part of the debtor to try to make an effort to pay off the debt. Put in at least three to four attempts per debtor. Of course, your goal is to try to get as large of a payment as possible out of the debtor as you can on each call you make. The best way to ensure you receive the payment on the call is to collect payment by credit card and process the payment right away. After making three to four attempts to collect on each file, reconvene with your client to see if they want you to continue trying to collect the debt. *Chapter 14 provides more information on setting up payment plans and agreements with clients.*

Making Effective Phone Calls

Use the following steps when making a phone call for collection:

- **Introduce yourself to the debtor:** As with collection letters, you must introduce yourself as a debt collector.

- **Call the place of employment:** If the debtor has provided a creditor with their work phone number, it is legal to contact him or her to recover an outstanding debt at work. If the debtor at any point requests the collection agency or creditor to not contact him or her at work, this must be honored.

- **Third-party communication:** If a debtor does not answer the phone, never divulge personal information or the reason for the call to a third party.

When calling a debtor, obviously you have no idea whom you are talking to, even if the person on the other end identifies himself or herself as the debtor. Validate whom you are talking to by informing him or her you are calling from a collection agency and which company you are representing. At this point, the person most likely will pause and listen intently or explain that he or she has no idea what you are talking about. Have a plan in action for each of those scenarios:

When the debtor pauses: Validate the person on the other end by asking for his or her full name, address, and Social Security number, and then quickly perform your job — recovering your client's money.

When the debtor "forgets" about their debt: Validate the person on the other end by asking for his or her full name, address, and Social Security number. Once you verify that you are speaking to the debtor, then quickly remind the debtor of the debt you are calling about by providing details, such as the purchase date, ending number of credit/debit card or checking account used, and the location of purchase.

Working with voice mails

As a collection professional, you sometimes will be talking to voice mails all day long. In doing so, do not forget the main rule, which is to protect the debtor's privacy. There is no way of knowing who will be listening to the voice mail. Therefore, messages must be as general as possible. Do not state that you are calling from a collection agency. Simply explain, "This is a very important message for [debtor's name]. It is urgent that you call us back today before 5 p.m." You can create a sense of urgency by giving a deadline for him or her to call you back. Most people will know by the nature of the message that it is a collection call and will either try to avoid you or dispute the debt if they think that it is not theirs.

Once a debtor has you on their radar, they tend to try to avoid your calls, so you may have to be crafty. For example, do not call them at or around the same time each day. Call them at different times that still fall in the legal hours you are able to contact them. Try not to show the phone number as unknown each time, and use different numbers, such as your business cell phone, the fax phone line, or even a home office line, to call the debtor, so they do not recognize the phone number.

Helping the Debtor Make a Decision

First, you have to listen. Listening with intent to resolve a situation with a little empathy and a lot of firmness puts you and the debtor in a mutually beneficial situation. Debtors tend to divulge enough information to help you help them make a decision, and they do not even realize they are doing it. For instance, if the debtor makes a statement that he or she only has $200 in his or her bank account, is unemployed, and waiting on a settlement to come in next month, your next step is to try to extract a payment today and possibly set up a payment plan. The scenario may sound like this:

Collection Rep: [State the name of the debtor], I can empathize with the fact that you are having financial difficulty, but ignoring this matter only causes the situation to snowball and make your situation worse. This debt is already 90 days past due, and it may affect your credit if you do not take care of it by paying it. I understand that you have $200 in the bank; making a minimum payment of only $50 today moves your account into a better standing, and then we can set up a payment plan to take care for the remaining balance. I can process this payment today. We accept check by phone, Visa˚, MasterCard, and Discover˚.

Debtor: Like I said earlier, I only have $200 available to me. My unemployment check barely covers my rent, and I will not begin receiving my settlement for a month.

Collection Rep: [State the name of the debtor], the debt definitively is not going away. While I respect your financial situation, a good faith payment of just $50 shows us that you do have interest in paying your bills. We also can set up a payment plan starting next month for once you begin receiving your settlement funds. How would you like to make the $50 payment today: by check or by credit or debit card?

Debtor: This sounds okay. I can pay via debit card.

The collection rep in the scenario above showed tenacity and empathy in helping the debtor to see the solution and recover the funds for the client. Always remember the bottom line is to recover the funds regardless of the debtor's situation. Your client is expecting you to do the job they hired you to do. And, your personal livelihood relies on your collecting as much money as possible.

You have the right to remain silent on a call

It is great to be ready with and knowledgeable on the facts for a collection call. However, in most cases, it is not necessary to divulge everything at once and then request payment on a debt. The person on the other end already knows what he or she owes and to whom and will typically do whatever it takes to stall on making a payment. Knowledge is power, but silence may be the key element to collecting on the debt. Ask a question that does not require a yes or no response. For example:

Q: *When will you be able to make a payment on this debt?*

Pause and do not say anything until the person on the other end responds. Many individuals do not expect or like to have dead air. Once the debtor responds, your next response and questions should feed off his or her answer. For example, if it is to set up a payment plan, *Chapter 14 provides the details on how to do handle this.*

Communicating Via Email

Communicating via email has its advantages and disadvantages. According to the CAN-SPAM Act, a consumer has to give you permission to contact them via email. If a debtor allows you to contact them by email, this does not mean that you should abandon trying to reach them by phone. The phone tends to be the most effective way to communicate with a debtor. A debtor may not check his or her email for weeks, but it is still a good tool to put in place because it provides written proof of the conversations you have with the debtor. Whether by phone or email, the debtor most likely still will try to stall, so always ask for a payment in your communication.

Many collection agencies do not believe in collecting via email because it can be too risky. Collecting through email leaves you open and vulnerable to lawsuits and complaints from debtors. However, the information you include in the email should be as simple as possible. Your goal is to keep the lines of communication open. You never have to divulge any details of the debt, payment plans, or settlements. Once you have initiated an email relationship and know that the debtor is available via email, you should lead him or her to contact you via phone so you can discuss the account and any arrangements in detail. Email communication is an option to use only if you deem it useful to your business. Making a rule to not communicate with a debtor via email may not have a substantial effect on the agency's recovery results.

Create a sense of urgency when sending email communications, just as you do when sending collection letters. In the first email, tell the recipient you need to hear from him or her by 5 p.m. today, or by Thursday at 5 p.m. — make sure you pick a firm deadline and stick to it. Stick to the goal at hand: collecting the money. If a person goes into a tirade about their issues, do not confirm the situation by elaborating on it; ask for the money and express that you understand and respect his or her situation, and then work out some type of a payment arrangement, just as you would during a phone conversation.

Keeping email communications legal

As with hard copy letters, email transmission must include the mini Miranda that informs debtors that you are a debt collector. Privacy is still a major issue. Email communication can easily get into the wrong in-box by transposing a few digits or letters. Always include a disclaimer at the bottom of the email:

Internet Email Confidentiality Statement

Information contained in this email message is intended only for the use of the individual to whom it is addressed and is private and confidential. If you have received this message in error, kindly destroy it and notify the sender immediately by reply email.

If you send three or more emails to the debtor without a response, and you are unable to get him or her on the phone, stop the email communication altogether. Either he or she has provided you with the wrong email address or will not respond to your inquiries.

Subject lines

Do not take subject lines lightly, as they are a major part of the communication process. Do not divulge any personal information in the subject line. Never express in the subject line that the email is about a debt. A good subject line may be, "Please call us today." This tells the reader there is important information he or she needs to acquire by calling. This may spark the recipient's curiosity as to what the nature of the email is about, which will make them more inclined to open the email. You do not want to come off threatening or demanding in your subject line. The subject line may get you the desired action — the recipient opening the email — but he or she might respond in a defensive manner, which will not help your attempts at collecting whatever outstanding debt he or she might have.

When You Have to Skip Trace

For many accounts you receive, the first step toward the collection process is actually to find the debtor. Even if the client provides details, such as the last known address, phone number, and email address of a debtor, you often will find that this has changed or is out of date. The art of finding a debtor or the assets of an individual or entity you are trying to collect a debt from is called skip tracing. There are different methods to pursue in order to find a person. However, the first step is to weigh the cost by deciding if the debt amount is worth spending an extensive amount of time or money on the process of locating the current whereabouts of the debtor. You may not know if you have to skip trace until after you have sent out initial collection letters; returned collection letters will trigger this.

Keep it simple — start in-house

When you decide to use the skip-tracing process to find a debtor, the best place to start is in-house. Use your own software and skills or those skills of your employees to try to find the debtor before outsourcing it to other companies. Each collection representative should try to skip trace on his or her accounts by:

- If the debtor's phone number has changed, check with your local 411 provider to find the new number. This may not always be successful because the person may have moved to another city, uses a cell phone, or has his or her number unlisted. However, it is a quick, simple, and feasible approach to start the process.

- If you have a valid phone number but no address, and the debtor keeps ignoring your calls, try using a reverse phone number lookup to get the new address of the person. Keep in mind that, again, the person may be using a cell phone or have his or her phone number private or unlisted. These services may have a minimal fee involved.

Reverse phone lookup resources

- o **www.whitepages.com/reverse_phone**
- o **www.reversephonedirectory.com** (also works with cell phones)
- o **www.reversephonelookupfree.com**

- If collection letters are being returned, the debtor may have moved. The postal service may provide you with the new forwarding address depending on how long ago the person has moved. You always can contact the postal service to obtain the forwarding address. The best way to obtain a change of address automatically is to use collection envelopes that say address change request on the outside, so the post office will automatically return this information to you when they return the piece of mail to you. There is an added cost for this service, but typically, it is worth it because it is a passive way to obtain the new address of a debtor. Or, check the white pages of your phone book for an updated address. Because many people have the same first and last name, keep the privacy rights laws in mind when you dial the number. Do your best to verify that you are talking to the actual debtor on the other end of the line before divulging any personal or debt information.

- Sometimes contacting a third party such as a neighbor or family member to verify a person's address can be helpful. Please keep in mind that, according to FDCPA, this is all you are able to do. Divulging any personal information or reason for looking for the person would be in violation of the law.

Using free online resources

The Internet has a host of options for trying to find someone. If you are not yet ready to spend the money on hiring a skip-tracing company, check the many free people finder resources available online. Most general searches are completely free. Some may require a nominal fee for providing additional information. Use the following list of sites to start your virtual skip trace:

- **www.411.com**
- **www.PhoneNumber.com**
- **www.Zabasearch.com**
- **http://Pipl.com**
- **www.123people.com**
- **www.ZoomInfo.com**
- **http://Skipease.com**

Social media networks may be worth trying, but as a collection professional, it is against the law to communicate with a debtor publicly about a debt. These networks include Facebook, Twitter, Myspace, and LinkedIn. If you do find a debtor on a social media network and the social media platform has a tool that allows you to send a private message to the debtor, then you can try contacting the debtor this way.

Outsourcing to skip-tracing pros

When your agency has depleted its in-house resources to find the debtor, you may require the help of a professional skip tracer. Multiple skip-tracing services are available. Your goal should be to find a respectable company that has a success rate. Because different skip-tracing companies provide different services, the rates will vary. To make sure you hire the right company, ask the following questions to narrow down your options:

1. What is the complete range of resources that you offer for skip tracing?
2. What service is included in each package you offer?
3. How many attempts do you make before closing a project?
4. What is your success rate for locating people?
5. Are there any additional fees that may be added with your services at any time?

Looking to private investigators

If the amount of debt owed is substantial, hiring a private investigator may be another option for finding a debtor. A private investigator is more ex-

pensive than hiring a typical skip-tracing company. However, private investigators have various tools and connections available to them to locate people. Make sure the investigator is licensed and understands the privacy and disclosure laws involved in finding and dealing with the debtor. Each state has a licensing board that governs the professional licensing of private investigators. There are many professional associations where you can find a qualified investigator, such as the Florida Association of Licensed Investigators (FALI): **www.fali.org**.

Summary

In order to get your client's debt paid, there must be a sense of urgency established throughout communication on the calls you have with debtors. Even while trying to find out who your contact person is, make a statement to the effect of their account could be suspended from receiving services. For example, if it is a credit card, then the credit card company may close the account, and the debtor will no longer be able to use his or her credit card. Also, explain to debtors that they might take a hit to their credit report if the debt is reported to the credit bureaus.

It is a good practice to find out if a person has personal liability to the debt before pursuing skip-tracing practices. If the debtor is not personally liable, nothing can be done to make them pay up. For example, if a person is an identity theft victim, has filed a police report, and can prove he or is a victim of fraud, he or she is not personally liable for the debt. Individuals who file for bankruptcy also may not be personally liable for repaying the debt. This is especially true when trying to collect debt incurred by a defunct business, which is one that has closed or has filed bankruptcy. The original principals of the company could very well have no personal liability. This will definitely put a damper on your ability to recover money for your client.

Chapter 13

Managing Customer Accounts — New and Old

Collection accounts, both new and old, are precious commodities to a collection agency. Having these accounts means that your marketing is effective in convincing clients that you are fully capable of collecting debt for them. Acquiring new accounts also means that clients are convinced that you are the right agency for them.

New Accounts: Protecting Sensitive Information

Throughout this entire book, protecting the rights of debtors has been a primary topic. Privacy becomes critical from the moment you first receive the account information from your client. There are different ways you can receive account information, such as via phone, mail, online, and worksheet transmitted by e-mail. Most collection agencies accept new accounts according to how the client wants to submit the information. Therefore, you most likely will be receiving debtor information in multiple ways. You should, however, have a system in place for each method.

- **Mail** — Your client may choose to submit collection account information in bulk via courier or parcel services provider. To make sure this sensitive information does not get into the wrong hands or is not improperly discarded, have a set time to pick up or drop off packages. If the client sends the information via United States Postal Service (USPS), find out how often or on what day these documents tend to be mailed, so the receptionist knows when to expect it.

- **Online** — If you allow online submission of account information, you have to make sure the website is secure. This means that you will have to invest money in software technology. If a hacker gets into your files and steals information, this could be a very costly mistake.

  On the other end of the account submission is the retrieval of information. Most likely, this information will be forwarded to a specific e-mail address. There needs to be a specific person(s) who is responsible for either distributing the information to the proper collection representative or to enter it into your collection software.

- **Worksheet** — Worksheet transmittals are ideal because you automatically receive multiple transactions at once that easily can be integrated in the system you are using. A good practice is to turn the worksheet into a password-protected file. You do not want anyone to have easy access to personal data that can be copied or saved easily.

- **Phone** — This form of new account information retrieval is the most time consuming and poses the most room for error. To prevent errors, such as writing down incorrect information, make sure representatives validate the information before hanging up the phone. This method is probably best suited when the client only has a few collection accounts to provide rather than a bulk amount.

Assigning them to a collection representative

Your company needs to have a plan in place to divide and assign accounts to collection representatives. Consider the amount of the debt, the age, and the client. These are key factors in deciding which accounts should be assigned to which representatives. Even if your agency has decided to divide the account by letters in the alphabet or by client, there are reasons to consider the above-mentioned categories, including:

- **Amount of Debt** — For some companies, a $2,000 account is a lot of money, and for others, it is not. You will know what a big- or small-dollar amount is for your agency. It may be best for a new or inexperienced collection representative to work with small accounts under the supervision of a more experienced employee. Larger debt accounts mean a larger payoff for the agency, so you want your best and most experienced representative on these accounts.

- **The Age of the Debt** — More experienced collection professionals — or even you — should handle any debt older than 180 days because it is a sensitive account. The longer an account remains outstanding, the less likely you are to collect on the debt. It is better to assign older accounts to more experienced collection representatives because it increases the likelihood the representative can collect on the account. A new or inexperienced collection representative might become too discouraged while pursuing this type of debt because the debtor has been able to avoid paying the debt for an extended period.

- **The client's status with your agency** — Each client is important to the overall success of your business. However, you must weigh the importance of the client. When their accounts attribute for a high portion of your profits, these clients should take priority over other clients. If you have one client that can make or break your business, put them into your own or the hands of your most qualified and trusted employee. This, however, should not be the only client you focus on, in case something happens to the relationship.

Communicating with your client

Clients tend to expect you to collect the funds on an account received today, yesterday. Unfortunately, the debt collection process takes time. Once you have entered pertinent data into the computer system, sent at least one collection letter, and made one phone call to the debtor, provide your client with a status report of the accounts they have sent to you. You can send the status report via e-mail, fax, or mail. A sample courtesy follow-up letter is below.

Dear [Insert the name of your client contact]:

Thank you for the recent collection accounts you placed with our agency. We take your business very seriously. This is a courtesy status report to inform you that we have begun the process necessary to collect on these accounts. Below you will find a complete list of your account placements and corresponding account numbers.

Name	Date Submitted	Account No.	Agency Account No.
Debtor	9.01.14	1234500	A46563
Debtor	9.01.14	5678900	A87650
Debtor	9.01.14	1011120	A27374

Please contact us at anytime with any questions you might have at (800) 000-0000. Once again, thank you for your business.

Sincerely,

Customer Service Team

When to start skip tracing

As discussed in Chapter 12, skip tracing well may be a part of validating new accounts. Just because a person does not pick up the phone or a call you back does not mean he or she is ignoring your call. It could mean that the client has provided you with outdated information. Start skip tracing when the collection letter is returned to you or you have left multiple messages with no response, a company has closed, or assets need to be located, so you can gain access to the assets to collect on a judgment, for example. When a legal collection judgment is filed, the client or the collection agency on behalf of the client can require the debtor to sell the assets or turn the assets over the creditor to sell to collect on the debt.

Managing Existing Accounts: When Accounts Get Stale

There will be times when you just cannot collect on an account. For instance, the debtor could be deceased, have left the country, have changed his or her identity, or could be good at avoiding his or her responsibilities. When you find that you have done everything you are legally capable of, your agency should schedule a meeting with the client to discuss the issues of the account. This is where documentation plays a vital role in your business. With your client, go over a timeline of actions taken to pursue recovery of the client's money. Also, inform them that you have used the best business practices with the case in question.

It is never a good idea to take advantage of a client's loyalty by pretending an account is going in a desired direction when it is not. Always consider your company's reputation in everything that you do. Telling a client that things are progressing well and then calling a meeting to explain that the account is uncollectible because you have not made any successful contact with the debtor will leave a bitter taste in the client's mouth, and they may very well pull all their accounts from you. Putting in a hard effort to collect and then being honest with your client, no matter the outcome, is the best policy.

A fresh look at a stale account

Before meeting with your client about a stale account, you may wish to have an in-house meeting. In this meeting, review the action taken to collect on the account and any responses from the debtor. Turn the meeting into a brainstorming session for staff members to provide input and suggestions on taking one last attempt to collect on the account. You can make the decision to transfer the account to another representative to have a new, fresh set of eyes working the account.

Using a tickler

The **aging report** is a report of old debt. It is a good tool to use to manage the agency's own accounts receivable as well. The aging report is like the Bible to making collection calls. Before making any phone calls, run a current aging report of all of the accounts you are planning to call or work. Most accounting software gives you the option to include as much search criteria as you want to narrow down your search. You can include the account holder's name, phone, Social Security number, balance, and original creditor and account number.

Criteria for a Commercial Aging Report
- Company name
- Address
- Phone number
- Contact person
- Invoice numbers
- Balance

Another great tool that agencies use to keep track of aging accounts is a tickler system. Tickler systems are like alarm clocks for your collection responsibilities. More specifically, a tickler is an application in debt software programs whereby you can set up specific reminders of important debt collection duties such as:

- A callback to a client to provide account updates
- Important deadlines for court filings
- A reminder to look for a promised payment from a debtor
- Calling a debtor on the due date to make a payment via phone

If this sounds a bit similar to using your Microsoft Outlook calendar, it is similar. However, tickler systems allow you to set the reminders with a little more ease. The account information already will be in front of you without any copying and pasting.

When to Report Debt to the Credit Bureau

At some point in the collection process, your only recourse is to report a debt to the credit bureau. This will not automatically ensure you will collect the funds, but it might prompt the debtor to begin making payments. It also might cause the debtor to understand the consequences of not paying his or her debt, which is that it can drag down their credit score. A poor credit score can prevent a person from getting loans for homes and cars, being able to rent an apartment, or even getting a job — so this gives you a little more power. Most people know that certain types of debt can be reported on their credit history for seven years. This means that it can prohibit the debtor from establishing new credit accounts when lenders and creditors see a collection account or bad debt on their credit.

When you see the debtor has no intention on paying off a debt — he or she is rude or avoiding all collection calls and letters, and he or she has not contested the debt — it is typically time to report the account to the credit bureaus. Many agencies have set periods for doing so. It is up to the client or the collection agency to set these periods. For example, most mortgage companies report a late mortgage payment to the credit bureaus when the payment is 30 days late. Other companies may wait 60, 90, 120, 180 or even more days of trying to collect on the debt before reporting it to the credit bureaus. The key to reporting to the credit bureau is making sure that you have followed the FCRA rules and regulations. Make sure have your facts straight:

- Do you have the correct spelling of the debtor's name?
- Do you have the correct social security number?
- Do you have the facts of the original debt, including the creditor, amount, and account number?
- Are you legally able to report on the debt? The original creditor may have to report the debt rather than the collection agency.

Once you know that you are in the right standing, you will have to follow the specific reporting procedures set forth by each of the three individual credit bureaus to which you are reporting. The three credit bureaus are Experian, TransUnion, and Equifax. Each credit bureau maintains its own records, so you or the original creditor will need to report to each credit bureau separately.

According to All Business, "To report a customer that is not paying, you first need to be a member of the proper credit agency. For a small fee, you can report delinquent accounts and gain access to credit reports. Equifax, Experian, and TransUnion handle reports for individuals."

About Credit Reports

Credit reporting means a creditor or collection agency reports information about a consumer's payment history to one or all three of the national reporting agencies, Equifax, TransUnion, or Experian. Not all companies report to all credit agencies. It depends on which credit bureau the company is a member of. Because each credit bureau keeps its own records, the payment history is reported to the bureau or bureaus to which the company reports. It is common for a company to be a member of only one credit bureau. The Fair Credit Reporting Act (FCRA) governs the three credit bureaus. As mentioned earlier, even though the act governs the reporting agencies, it is still a good idea for you to familiarize yourself with the act. The credit report can benefit you more than allowing you to update information to a debtor's account. During the collection process, you can glean vital information from a debtor's credit report that may aid you in performing your collection duties. Some of the information you can discover from a credit report includes:

- Personal identification information
- Credit account information
- Inquiries from other lenders and creditors inquiring about the debtor's credit history
- Public record information, such as mortgages, tax liens, and contractor's liens

According to information provided by Experian, there are two types of inquiries on a credit report. There are those that potential creditors are able to see; and others those only consumers are able to see. Consumers are protected in many ways; so the FCRA prohibits credit reporting agencies from storing certain information such as bank account information, credit risk scores, medical information, purchase transaction and history, or criminal background. Much of this information may not be of importance to the success of debt recovery except possibly the bank account information of the debtor.

Where information comes from

The information noted on a consumer's credit report comes from multiple sources. Just as your client reports payment and default information on the debtor to the credit bureaus, so do other credit account companies, lenders, and other companies. By law, however, the information reported on a credit report can come only from specific sources, which include:

Creditors — Creditors can provide the credit reporting agency with specific data about their customers such as credit limit, loan amount, the open date of the account, amount of the monthly payments, status of payments/account, balance, payment history.

Public Records — Credit reporting agencies routinely collect public data on consumers from state and federal court records. This data includes items such as judgments, bankruptcies, and tax lien records.

Inquiries — The credit reporting agency captures data from companies reviewing a consumer's credit data. This information remains on a credit report for a specific period.

Statements from Consumers — A credit report obtains information from consumers. These statements include account disputes, employment status, and personal contact information, such as a mailing or living address.

The law requires that certain information can remain on an individual's credit account for a specified time. Your new agency needs to familiarize itself with this information on collection accounts.

Chapter 13 bankruptcy	7 years
Chapter 7 bankruptcy	10 years
Civil judgments	7 years
Closed accounts (in good standing)	10 years
Collection accounts	7 years
Credit inquiries	2 years
Late or missed payments	7 years
Open accounts (in good standing)	Indefinitely
Tax liens (paid)	7 years
Tax liens (unpaid)	10 years

What Clients Expect from a Collection Agency

Customer service is still an important aspect of doing business. Every customer has expectations. It is your responsibility to run your business in a manner conducive to top-tier customer service standards. When a new client reaches out to your collection agency, it is essential that you anticipate the client's needs. Pay close attention to their conversation to provide them with services they need.

Summary

It is important to understand that a client has thousands of collection agencies to choose from to work on its accounts. To ensure that there is a smooth transition from account acquisition and satisfaction, your agency should have a detailed, strategic plan in place for team members to practice.

When the client has a question about any report from the agency, prompt and accurate communication is what they expect from you. Even if you are unable to answer an inquiry right away, at least inform the client that you are seeking the right answer and will get back with them within a certain amount of time. You will have the opportunity to become an integral part of your client's business.

Clients expect honesty and trustworthiness from a collection agency. You will be dealing directly with another company's money, so they have put a lot of trust in your agency. Always tell clients the truth and ensure that all collected funds owed make it into the client's hands promptly and accurately by using direct deposit to transfer the funds, you collect from your business bank account to your client's bank account.

Chapter 14

Payment Plans, Settlements, and Getting Paid

n a perfect world, clients would make purchases on credit or with a loan and make their credit or loan payments on time to the company. If this were the case, however, there would be no need for collection agencies. The collection process can be a win-win situation if you take the time to conduct some research on the financial situation of the debtor you are trying to collect from in the first place. If the person had the money to make the payments, he or she most likely would be paying them, and you would not even know the person existed. It is all about the approach you take to collect on the debt. When you take the time to find out a little more about the debtors' financial situations, you can decipher how much money they may be able to pay on weekly, biweekly, or monthly payment plans.

Put it in Writing

As soon as you come to a payment arrangement with a debtor on the phone, you want to document your agreement in writing. You can create a form letter for payment arrangements ahead of time and fill in the details of the arrangements on your computer before mailing it out or e-mailing it out to the client. Remember to request a response to your letter or e-mail that confirms the debtor's understanding and affirmation of the agreement.

Having the agreement in writing helps confirm the debtor's personal liability to the debt, and making even one payment on the plan puts the agency in a good position because it lowers the total outstanding balance the creditor is owed. If the debtor does not adhere to the payment agreement, the client can file suit against the debtor. In this case, a judgment is placed on the debtor, the courts can force the debtor to pay by garnishing their payroll checks for the payments or requiring the debtor to pay the court, and then the court pays the creditor. *Garnishing is further explained in Chapter 15.*

Once payment plans are in place, enforce them. Going back on an original agreement will make the debtor believe you are not serious about your business, and he or she will continue to take advantage of the situation. In addition to the original payment arrangement agreement you send to the client, it is a good time to touch base with the client via phone or a payment reminder letter as the first payment due date and each subsequent payment due date approaches.

A sample payment arrangement agreement should be on your collection agency letterhead and may read as follows:

September 1, 2014

Jane Jones
12345 ABC St.
Anytown, USA 11111

RE: Account Number: 12345
       Amount Due: $2,897.15
       Claimant: XYZ Widget Co.

This agreement serves as confirmation that you have agreed to pay on the above-mentioned debt.

As agreed upon, you will make six payments of $482.85. The due date of each payment is on the 5th of each month. The payment schedule is as follows:

- Payment 1: Due October 5, 2014

- Payment 2: Due November 5, 2014

- Payment 3: Due December 5, 2014

- Payment 4: Due January 5, 2015

- Payment 5: Due February 5, 2015

- Payment 6: Due March 5, 2015

Please sign the extra copy of the enclosed agreement and return it to us in the postage-paid envelope. If we do not receive the signed agreement within 15 days of sending the notice, then further collection actions will proceed.

Sincerely,

Katie D. Collector

X _____

Easy Payment Options

In the past, sending a self-addressed envelope and a bill was convenient for businesses and consumers. Now, we can expedite the payments, which make your life, the life of the debtor, and the lives of your clients a lot easier. Now, payment options include e-checks, credit cards, and debit cards. If you are collecting on bad credit card debt, you should require the debtor pay off the debt using another payment method:

- E-check via phone or online
- Western Union
- Money order

Offering Settlements on Balance Due

You will come across some debtors who are willing to negotiate a complete payoff on their debt if you are willing to negotiate the total amount they have to pay, as seen in the example in Chapter 10. For example, if they have a credit card balance of $15,000, they may be willing to pay the whole thing off immediately if you cut their balance by 30 percent. In the collection business, this is a settlement. You are settling the debt account by taking less than the total amount due. Settlements are not made in payments. Settlements require the client to pay the settled-upon amount in one lump sum amount.

Typically, you and your client have discussed how much flexibility you have to negotiate settlement amounts. You also should consider that when you settle for an amount that is less than what is due, you are cutting your commission. You should consider, however, that less of a commission is better than no commission at all. So, typically, if you can get the client to settle within the parameters you and the client have discussed ahead of time, it is better than not being able to close the debt out altogether.

Communicating the Settlement Offer to the Debtor

If you have exhausted all of your efforts to collect the full amount due, but the debtor is willing to make a lump-sum payment at a reduced total balance, you can send a settlement agreement that states this. Inform the debtor that the agency is willing to accept a percentage of the total amount due, and note the expiration date of the offer. Generally, 14 to 30 days from receipt of the agreement is the average time for a debtor with a lump-sum payment agreement. You can find a sample offer notice below. If a debtor does not respond or take you up on the offer, the settlement is void, and the debt reverts to the original balance due.

Sample Settlement Notice

ABC Collection Agency and [Insert name of client] have agreed to the settlement amount of $1,896, which represents 60% of the amount currently owed on the XYZ Credit Account. Full payment is due no later than thirty (30) days from receipt of this notice or the settlement offer is considered null and void and the debt amount returns to the original balance due.

Debtors know and expect that collection agencies will offer settlements during tax season. This is an opportune time, as tax returns put a little discretionary income in the hands of debtors. Take advantage of this time and begin working on settlement offers on extremely outstanding accounts a couple weeks before tax season arrives.

Reporting Settlements to Credit Bureaus

When you reach a settlement with the debtor and the debtor has paid the settlement amount as agreed, you should report this to each of three credit bureaus that you have previously recorded the outstanding debt. This changes the collection account now showing on the debtor's credit report to a settled account, which shows future creditors that the debtor did take care of paying off the account. Take the following steps to ensure smooth completion and closure of a settlement:

1. Once you receive the full settlement payment from the debtor, send them a letter confirming the payment was received, and their account now has a zero balance.

2. Notify the credit bureaus in writing that the account is paid in full via settlement.

Getting Paid and Making a Profit

Pricing is one of the most important aspects of the collection businesses because it will affect your income and the budget you have to market and promote your service. As the agency owner, you will be responsible for developing and negotiating the price of your services with your clients. New business owners tend to price themselves out of a new account by reaching too high or too low. Potential clients have done their research to see what the average going rate is to place their accounts with a collection agency. If your price is far below the average, the prospect may assume you are new and too inexperienced to handle their accounts even if you have years in the collection industry. What tends to happen if you price too low is that you are not being paid what you are worth. The best thing to do is to research your competition up front. Your research should include collection agencies that cover your specific niche, geographic region, or any other services in which you specialize. Price your services according to the going rate, but also consider your experience, the number of years your collection agency has been open, and the rate your competition is charging. This tends to keep you from pricing your services too high or too low, but rather somewhere fair and in between.

Steps to receive payment for the debt collected

How your agency receives payment for your services is based upon what you agree to with your clients. And will depend on how you are billing the client (such as commission or flat fee). Some options for charging clients include:

- **Automatic Deduction** — With agreement from your customer, your agency may collect the debt amount from the debtor, deduct your commission from the amount collected, and then submit the difference to the client. It is important to keep this information organized, especially if you are receiving different commissions for different types or quantities of debt. Be able to provide the client with a detailed account of what was received from debtors, the amount the agency was paid, and the total actually paid to the client for each account. Provide the client with these details each time you process a payment for them.

- **Vendor Management System (VMS)** — Some companies use vendor management systems (VMS). These systems are used to track and pay all their vendors. Using these systems may require a little work on your part to get paid, as you may have to submit manual or electronic invoices. You also may have to wait for approval in the system before receiving payment.

- **Weekly or Monthly Spreadsheet Submission** — In some cases, you might have to submit a spreadsheet of transactions and what is owed to you to the accounts payable department in order to receive your payment. Once again, make sure to provide detailed information. If the accounts payable person has a problem with your numbers or information, they may return the spreadsheet to you for correction, which delays your payment.

- **Invoice** — Your agency can invoice your client normally and wait to receive your payment in the mail.

If you come to a settlement agreement with a debtor, where they pay 60 percent of the debt, your commission is adjusted accordingly. For example, if you originally were to be paid 30 percent of a $10,000 debt, but the debtor pays $6,000, then you will receive 30 percent of the $6,000, which is $1,800 instead of $3,000. The same is true if you get the debtor to agree to monthly payments. You will receive your commission based on the monthly payment amount.

Summary

When you are negotiating with debtors, your goal is one of two choices. You either want to get them to agree to make payments, or you want to reach a lump-sum payoff. If you do make payment arrangements with the client, collect the first payment while you are still on the phone. Put all agreements in writing and enforce the agreement you have come to with debtors, no matter what the terms and conditions are.

Collection is a service that requires performance in order to receive payment. Therefore, most prospects expect not to pay anything until you actually have collected on the debt. Because it is a commission-based environment, you may not be able to publish any rates because you and your competitors may charge different rates based upon the type of collection, the amount to be collected, and the location. You also may negotiate different rates with different clients based on myriad factors. You are the only person who knows what it costs to run your business, so you must consider this when deciding on your fees. Based on these facts, you will find that some accounts are not worth your time. It is better to know this up front instead of wasting your time talking about accounts that will not benefit you. Time is really money in this industry; any time not spent collecting on accounts must be justified.

Chapter 15

Lawsuits, Complaints, and Legal Counsel

After doing all that you can to recover outstanding debt, you might have to call in a stronger force — an attorney. There are things to consider before taking this route, such as the amount of the outstanding debt, the complexity of the case, and the personal liability of the debtor. Depending on how complex the case, the creditor might be able to file suit with the court on their own behalf. However, if this will take away too much of the agency's time to pursue other recovery activities, the support of an attorney is necessary. Other reasons to get an attorney involved include:

- When you have filed suit and the debtor has hired an attorney to represent them

- When the debtor has filed a counterclaim

- When the debtor has signed affidavits from family members claiming harassment or disclosure of debtor's personal information

Lawsuits can quickly snowball, even if it seems like a simple case and you have followed the rules with certainty you are in the right. It is even a

good idea to have an attorney review your case before filing a suit to see what legal measures can be pursued to help recover a debt without involving the court system.

Choosing to File Suit against a Debtor

If a consumer or debtor leaves you with no other choice but to file suit, do it aggressively, expeditiously, and within the federal and state laws governing the industry. Therefore, you must weigh the options, and be sure you want to take this step. After brainstorming with your client, your client may find that writing off a debt is the best avenue for a five-year-old, $1,000 debt owned by a marginally employed person who moves around and changes phone numbers frequently. It might cost the agency more to file suit against the debtor than to forgive the debt in the first place. Forgiveness of a debt means that the company erases it, as if it never existed, and the creditor no longer takes any measures to try to collect on it.

Naming the best strategy

Just because you know the debtor owes does not mean you have a good court case. In order to make sure you have a fair chance of winning, discuss these things with your attorney:

- Whether the person you are suing has personal liability
- Documentation of all collection attempts and actions taken

- The strengths and weaknesses of the claim
- The defendant: individuals, spouses, principals of a company, or the company

Once you have your causes of action together and all the details of the case, you or your attorney must file the necessary documentation with the court. Remember that filing charges can differ according to what you are filing, such as the amount of money you are suing for and the number of defendants. This is important information to keep track of, as you want to include these fees and any attorney fees in your lawsuit to add on to the amount the debtor owes you and/or your client. When your client wins a court case against a debtor, the client also can sue for all of the fees involved in having to take the debtor to court.

Debt collector rights when it comes to garnishing

If your agency has to take a debtor to court on a creditor's behalf, it is important to keep in mind there is a possibility you might not receive the money owed, even if a judgment is made in your favor. There will be cases when a debtor is **judgment-proof**. This means that a creditor or their representing collection agency cannot secure money from a debtor that is insolvent, lacks enough property to satisfy the debt, or is in some way protected by laws that prohibit wages and property from being used to satisfy a claim. On the other hand, if it has been determined that a person is not judgment-proof, according to the FTC, a creditor or debt collector may garnish a debtor's wages or bank account. **Garnishing** occurs when a person has money involuntarily and legally taken from them due to funds owed to another party such as the government or creditor.

The suing agency and their attorney will have to submit the proper documents to the court to request that the debtor's wages be garnished. If it is approved, the debtor's employer automatically will withhold a portion of the debtor's compensation to pay off the judgment. There are limitations when it comes to federal benefits because some are exempt from being garnished. The benefits that may be excluded from garnishment include, but are not limited to:

- Social Security benefits
- Supplemental Security Income (SSI) benefits
- Veterans' benefits
- Civil Service and Federal Retirement and Disability benefits
- Service members' pay
- Military annuities and survivors' benefits
- Student assistance
- Railroad retirement benefits
- Merchant seamen wages
- Longshoremen's and Harbor Workers' Death and Disability benefits
- Foreign Service Retirement and Disability benefits
- Compensation for injury, death, or detention of employees of U.S. contractors outside the U.S.
- Federal Emergency Management Agency Federal Disaster Assistance

When the Debtor Sues

As a collection agency owner, you might find yourself in court pursuing debtors, but you also may find yourself on the opposite side of the courtroom when consumers decide to fight back. Since the recession began in 2007, the number of consumer lawsuits against collection agencies has increased by nearly 40 percent. As the amount of debt increases, collection professionals are trying to pursue debtors more aggressively. However, as a business owner, you should monitor your staff and ensure their desire to collect on the debt does not cloud their judgment for following the rules.

You may not be able to hire an attorney to have on retainer, but it is a good idea to do your research now and find out which attorneys work collection agency cases. Also, find out the success rate for these particular lawyers. Your experienced colleagues will know which attorneys are best in your town. Take some time to ask around and get feedback before making any permanent decisions. You also should check with the bar association in your state to find out more details on attorneys.

There are many reasons for a consumer to file a lawsuit against a collection agency, including harassment and threats, or because the person has explained that he or she is not the owner of a debt, such as a victim of identity theft who has a police report and documentation. According to the FTC, a consumer has the right to sue a debt collector in state or federal court within one year of the FDCPA rule or regulation being violated. If the debtor wins the case, the debt collector will have to pay the debtor for proven damages, such as lost wages or medical bills caused by the illegal collection practices. Furthermore, a judge reserves the right to require the debt collector to pay the debtor up to $1,000 even if the debtor is unable to prove actual damages, and the debtor can be reimbursed for attorney's fees and court costs.

The law also allows class-action lawsuits (multiple debtors suing at one time) that can recover damages up to $500,000 or one percent of the collection agency's net worth; whichever of the two amounts is lower. One thing to keep in mind is that just because the debtor has won a lawsuit based upon the collection agency failing to follow collection practices law does not mean the debtor is not obligated to pay their debt.

As previously noted, you should be recording notes in the file of each debtor, so if a lawsuit ensues, you will have all of the background information on your actions that the client can use in court. For example, a debtor may claim harassment when your representative only might have called the debtor twice in two days. You or your collection representatives will be able to identify debtors that could potentially turn into problems. As you are performing your normal phone call documentation, highlight complaints that accuse the agency of breaking collection laws. This should be done even if the debtor has not threatened to file a lawsuit. As the agency owner, you can have a bimonthly or quarterly meeting to review these types of complaints and to scrutinize how the debtor really is being treated. This is important because a suing debtor inevitably will be building a case against you. The debtor initially will ask you stop calling and follow up with a certified letter. In addition, the debtor will build his or her case by getting others involved who might have witnessed the collection agency's actions; these witnesses may provide affidavits. At this point, your agency should have all the facts available to certify the validity of the debt. You should run the possibility of a debtor lawsuit by your lawyer to get legal input on where you stand on protecting your company. Thinking ahead and putting your documentation together before a lawsuit helps you and your attorney prepare in the case of legal actions.

Below is a summarization of just a couple of lawsuits filed against debt-collection agencies. This will provide you with a picture of what debtors sue for and how much they were awarded when they won.

Case I

In 2008, a collection agency and its owners paid $2.25 million to settle charges that the agency's collectors violated the FTC and FDCPA laws and regulations while collecting debt. The Department of Justice (DOJ) filed a complaint on the FTCs behalf charging that the collection agency allowed their agency collectors to execute unlawful collection practices including:

- False or deceptive threats of garnishment, arrest, and legal action
- Improper calls to consumers
- Frequent, harassing, threatening, and abusive calls
- Unfair and unauthorized withdrawals from consumers' bank accounts
- Failing to adequately investigate consumer complaints or discipline collectors

- Rehiring of those debt collectors who had previously violated the FDCPA

Case II

The FTC filed a complaint against a collection company and two of its principals for trying to collect on debt not owed by a consumer without reporting to the credit-reporting agency that the consumer disputed the debt. In addition, the collection company continued to assert that consumers owed debt that had already been paid off.

This collection company agreed to pay $1 million dollars to settle these charges.

Case III

In March of 2004, a collection agency was ordered to pay $1 million to settle charges filed by the FTC that the company and its principals violated federal collection practices by threatening and harassing thousands of consumers and trying to force them to pay debts that had reached the statute of limitations or on debts not owed. The companies and the principals paid a $300,000 civil penalty and were barred from engaging in future deceptive, abusive, and illegal collection practices.

Later, in December of 2004, the FTC sued this same company and its principals and alleged that they continued to intimidate, harass, and use deceptive debt collection methods to try to collect debt beyond the statute of limitations or on debt not owed at all. The court entered a temporary restraining order, froze the defendants' assets, and appointed a receiver to oversee the company and its assets. Essentially, the receiver shut the company down. The settlement also included:

- Barring the defendants from performing debt collection activities or helping others engaged in debt collection activities

- Forcing the defendants to pay the FTC $1 million in ill-gotten gains

The above cases show the types of legal cases your collection agency may face. This helps you understand the importance of having a compliance plan in place for all levels of staff within your agency. Each member of your agency working with consumers must have access to FDCPA statutes and any other collection laws your state has incorporated.

Also, the more information consumers receive about collection laws and how to protect themselves, the more empowered they become. Even if they are not certain if they actually have a case, consumers may sue. This should not hinder you from operating or starting an agency, just ensure you conduct your collections ethically and within the measure of the law. Every business and industry faces the possibility of being sued by its customers or clients and continues to thrive.

Consumer Complaints

Consumers have the right to pursue complaints on debt collectors if they feel their rights have been violated. Even if the collection agency has not broken the law, a consumer complaint will shine a bright light on the agency. The collection agency has to be prepared to defend its actions with detailed accounts of its encounters with the consumer. Furthermore, the agency will need to explain that they have a compliance plan in place that enforces the FDCPA laws and regulations as the foundation for how it communicates with consumers.

A consumer can file a complaint on a collection agency in three different ways:

- Complain to the Federal Trade Commission (**www.ftccomplaintassistant.gov**)

- Complain to the state attorney general
  (**www.naag.org/current-attorneys-general.php**)
- Complain to the Better Business Bureau (**www.bbb.org**)
  - o   The Better Business Bureau is not a government entity and has no legal recourse to pursue any legal actions against a collection agency. The BBB does keep complaints on record, so clients researching doing business with your company may decide not to if you have too many complaints against you.

Each agency performs its own investigation and tries to gather information from both the creditor and the debtor. In some cases, fines may be assessed or a record of complaints is kept on file, which can prevent other clients from hiring your collection agency.

Dispute letter

Once again, consumers are well-informed of their rights as it pertains to debt collection. The FTC has put several guidelines in place to help consumers work through the debt collection process in a manner that does not help them escape from their debt but have peace and sanity during the process. A sample letter you may receive from a consumer is noted below.

In the mini Miranda, discussed in Chapter 14, there is a notification that the consumer must contact the collection agency within 30 days. In the past, many consumers ignored this statement and called the agency to state the debt did not belong to them. This is not the case anymore, so it is important that you pay attention to all mail sent to your agency. Some will contain a debt dispute letter, which, if not addressed, can cause additional issues.

<u>**CERTIFIED MAIL**</u> — **RETURN RECEIPT REQUESTED**

ABC Collection Agency
1 Collection Drive, Suite 5D
Recovery City, FL 32839

RE: 77771

Dear ABC Collection Agency:

This dispute letter is in response to the communication sent by your agency on Aug. 1, 2014, stating that I have an outstanding debt in the amount of $800 owed to World Electric.

I am disputing this debt and have legal rights to do so under the Fair Debt Collections Practice Act. The law requires that you cease collection efforts unless you have validated the debt as belonging to me.

Please provide me with the following information:

- Name, address, and phone number of the creditor.

- Detailed proof that the debt belongs to me. Acceptable information includes an invoice or statement from the creditor detailing the exact amount of the original debt, the original account number, and all payments made on the account.

Until this information is verified, I am requesting that you do not contact me any further. If for any reason that you are not able to validate this data, please inform the credit bureaus of this finding.

Any additional communication from your agency is limited to your findings via written documentation that proves this debt belongs to me.

Sincerely,

Mr. Debtor

If you do find that the debt does not belong to the debtor, then collection efforts stop. In the status update reports to your client, you would let them know that the debt is not valid. Collection agents only are paid on debt that is collected, so if the debt is invalid, then you will not be paid for trying to collect the debt.

Collection in the Media: How to Respond to Reporters

In Chapter 2, there was mention of the state of the collection industry. It seems as if the media is producing horror stories about people having poor dealings with collection agencies. The media cannot be blamed for this; a few bad agencies are making the entire industry look bad. The stories about what consumers are going through are horrific, and sometimes you have to ask if they are exaggerated. Nonetheless, it is a poor reflection on the industry and because you soon will be operating in this industry, you must understand what is going on and why. First, nothing gains attention like fraud, finances, and consumer bullying.

Your compliance plan and training are put in place to ensure ethics in your establishment. One way to avoid being thrown into the spotlight is to put a great emphasis on this plan and have a zero-tolerance policy for all employees when it comes to following the law. If the media gets wind of multiple consumer complaints against your collection agency, they may come knocking at your door. When this happens, take the following measures to protect your agency.

1. Speak to your attorney.
2. Monitor your collection representatives' calls to make sure everyone is in compliance.
3. Speak to your staff to find out any issues they are having with accounts.
4. Speak to your public relations representative to provide you with a statement if they deem it necessary.

Work with the media

One of the best things that you can do for your business is to build a relationship with the media. Reporters always are looking for reliable sources to help them with stories. One way to make your agency available is to contact the local reporter that reports on consumer protection and offer to help with his or her next story. The reporter may want you to give input on current problems that consumers are facing.

Summary

After watching any television court shows, you may feel that you have what it takes to take on a debtor yourself. However, things can get complicated fast, and lack of information, knowledge, or your inability to answer a judge's question swiftly and with confidence can make winning your case all the more difficult. Always consider the benefits of consulting with an attorney for all possible lawsuits. Lawsuits against debtors should be a last resort after exhausting all other efforts.

Even if you have a great compliance plan and a zero tolerance policy for your employees, things can go wrong. There are times when debtors make false allegations against collection agencies. Either way, you may find yourself fighting against debtors in the courtroom, which is why it is important that you have a competent legal team or a creditable attorney on your side.

When the media reports on cases involving collection agencies, everyone will want to listen to find out who the culprit is and how he or she can protect him or herself and those around from dealing with the bad business. The collection industry has become the favorite industry to write about; even with all of the laws in place to keep agencies in line, many tend to go astray. Collection is a respectable field, and you should be proud of what you are doing if you uphold the high standards of an ethical collection agency. You not only are helping companies keep up with their cash flow, but you also are helping debtors to finally relieve some of the stress that has been weighing them down.

Chapter 16

The Future of your Successful Business – Franchising, Selling, or Closing

ranchised businesses are individually-owned businesses that are operated under the name and rules of a large chain, called the franchisor. If your collection agency is operating successfully, consistently brings in a substantial profit, and could expand, you may have an interest in franchising your collection agency. In this case, you would sell the rights of others to use your model of starting and operating the collection agency according to your model, rules, and regulations. The franchisee, or person who purchases a franchise, pays you for the use of all of this information. To turn your business into a franchise requires a lot of preparation work on your part to implement everything from operating procedures to duplicating every step of your business model, so the franchisee can start and operate as successful a collection agency as you have. This means you have to test, retest, and develop a written standard manual that covers the best business practices from startup to profit bearing. When you sell a franchise, you receive upfront payments from the buyer of the franchisee, and you even can receive a percentage of the franchise business on an ongoing basis.

Let a Franchisee Find You

There are various ways to find places to sell your franchise opportunities. Prospects can search online for "collection agency franchise businesses." Franchise websites, such as Franchise Opportunities (**www.franchiseopportunities.com**) and Franchise Gator (**www.franchisegator.com**) help to match franchisors with franchisees. Additionally, *Entrepreneur* magazine provides a list of the top 200 franchised businesses and sells ad space where

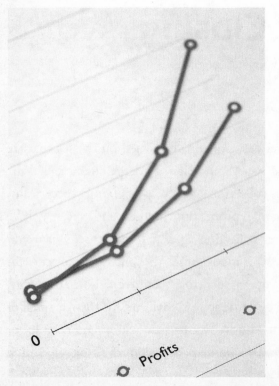

you can promote your franchise opportunity.

Other ways to promote your collection agency franchise is to participate in franchise trade shows, seminars, and conferences. You may consider renting a booth or serving as a speaker. Just as you aggressively promoted your company in the startup and growth stages, the same tenacity is required to convince franchisees that you have a quality, profitable business to franchise. Knowledge and information is key to a potential buyer, so be prepared to provide prospects with as much information as possible so they can make an informed decision.

Do not make the mistake of thinking the person on the other end of the sale is only becoming an extension of your business; they are buying their own business opportunity but following your business model, as you have built a successful one. To make the most of your expo experience, consider creating a list of questions and comments that potential franchisees will be asking you, so you are prepared to respond in an appropriate and productive manner.

Some questions franchisees may ask you include:

- How long has the company been in business?
- How many franchisees does the company currently have? How many are in your area?
- Is the area I am interested in available? If not, what areas are available?
- What are the costs, including the initial cost to purchase the franchise, the royalties, and the marketing fees?
- How do the royalty fees work, and how long do I pay them?
- Are the royalty fees a percentage of sales or a set fee?
- What is the marketing fee?
- What assistance will the franchisor provide to me as a franchisee? Is the assistance given just during the startup phase or on a consistent basis?
- How much control do I have as a franchisee on what services I provide or how I run my business?
- Can I speak to an existing owner (which they already might be doing)?

The Grilling Process:
Investigating the Franchisor

Buying a franchise is a huge financial commitment. If you decide to franchise your agency, be prepared to be investigated thoroughly. So, the first thing that you must do is to hire a lawyer to help you with all of the legal aspects.

The first task is developing a franchisors disclosure document. This document is required by the FTC and must be provided to the prospective franchisee ten business days before he or she signs papers or money is transferred to buy the franchise. This is done so that people are not pressured into signing contracts, and they have plenty of time to review the documents, talk with their attorneys, and do any research to understand the details of the deals.

The disclosure document, called the Uniform Franchise Offering Circular (UFOC), is supplied to prequalified franchisees. They are available online, are typically about 50 pages long, and will include many details. The entire document can be viewed as a Microsoft Word document online at **www. nasaa.org/content/Files/UniformFranchiseOfferingCircular.doc**. This document is supplied by the North American Securities Administrators Association (NASAA), which outlines information including:

- Franchisor name
- Business experience of key officials
- Litigation record
- Bankruptcy record
- Initial franchise fee
- Other fees
- Initial investment, including franchise fee, equipment, and any other costs
- Any requirements about where to purchase products and services
- Franchisee's obligations

- Franchisors' obligations
- Territories, including exclusivity and growth options
- Trademarks
- Patents, copyrights, and property information
- Obligation to participate in operating the business
- Restrictions on what franchisee may sell
- Contract renewal, termination and transfers, and dispute resolution
- Earnings claims — estimates of what the franchisee may earn
- List of all franchise outlets, with contact names and numbers
- Franchisor's audited financial statements
- Receipt — signed proof that prospective franchisee received UFOC
- Use of public figures — payment to celebrities or high-profile persons and/or their investment into the system

Franchise financing

Most people interested in franchising your agency will not have the money to pay for it outright or pay all of your fees up front. Fortunately, you can provide plenty of resources to potential franchisees to come up with the money they need to invest in your franchise. One option is the International Franchise Association (**http://franchise.org**), which lists more than 30 franchise lenders. Also, the U.S. Small Business Administration (**www.sba.gov**) works with banks using guaranteed loan programs for startup franchisees. Lenders have discovered the potential for growth and stability within the franchise market and are willing to look at financing these ventures.

Preparing to Leave Your Business

At some point in the future, you either will want to move on to another business, retire from the collection business, or otherwise leave your business for some reason. If you plan to sell your business, it is imperative to be able to show that your collection business is profitable and productive.

Most business experts suggest that when you are going through the process of planning your business, you should also have a plan in place to exit it.

An Exit Plan

Now is the time to develop an exit plan for your collection business. You will not need as much detail for the exit plan as you needed for your original business plan, but you will want to develop it now and review it each year so you can make any changes necessary. Your business situation inevitably will change from year to year, and you will want to revise your exit plan. Here are some of the basic items your plan should cover:

- **Your best-case scenario:** Do you know when you want to retire? Decide whether you want to sell the business or leave it for your family to manage.

- **Current value:** If you were to sell your business today, what is it worth?

- **Enhancing business value:** What changes would make your business more appealing for a buyer? Consider these carefully, and realize that there might be some changes you do not necessarily want to make but that will enhance the value of the business when it is time to sell.

- **Worst-case scenario:** If you had to get out of the business today, what could be done?

- **Preparing for the sale:** You will want to be aware of the tax implications of the sale.

- **Leaving:** Are you in a partnership or corporation with others, and if so, how does this affect how you leave your business?

- **Financial health for your family:** Prepare a will. Is your family trained and prepared to run the business without you?

It is recommended that you meet with your attorney and your CPA (for tax ramification purposes) for advice about how to create a realistic exit plan. To see some examples of exit plans, go to:

- American Express° Small Business:
  www.americanexpress.com/smallbusiness
- Principal Financial Group°:
  www.principal.com/businessowner/bus_exit.htm
- Family Business Experts:
  www.family-business-experts.com/exit-planning.html

Leaving Your Business to a Family Member

Millions of large and small businesses are operated by families. Some owners pass their business down to family members or heirs.

There are tax implications if you leave the business to a family member, such as inheritance tax, trusts, and tax-free gifts, which the recipient is responsible for paying. Each of these issues is complicated, and you should consult with your attorney, banker, estate planner, and CPA on these matters. Additional resources for information include:

- U.S. Chamber of Commerce offers advice at
  www.uschamber.com.
- CCH° Business Owner's Toolkit has articles to help you at
  www.toolkit.com.

Selling to Your Employees

You might not have family members who are interested in carrying on the business without you, so you might consider selling the business to your employees. They would need to have adequate financing; so, you should make it a professional transaction and include your attorney or accountant in the process. Be aware that this can be highly emotional, as the employees buying your business might have different plans and ideas for how to "change" your business. The other issue is that it might feel uncomfortable to negotiate money issues with people that have previously worked side-by-side with you and even reported to you as their boss.

Your employees might want to talk with a professional so they clearly understand the transaction. For advice, see:

- The National Center for Employee Ownership at **www.nceo.org**
- The Foundation for Enterprise Development at **www.fed.org**

There are many ways to handle this transaction, including transferring your business to a worker co-op or transferring directly to employees, similar to transferring it to family members. You should obtain advice and understand the process for everyone's sake.

Summary

Trying to franchise, sell, or close a collection business can be difficult when it comes to pricing because most pricing is based on percentages of different debt amounts, which in a collection business is commissioned based. However, you should work with an attorney, tax expert, and a franchise expert to help you evaluate how much you can sell your business for as a franchise. An attorney and tax professional can help you determine the value of the business if you choose to sell the business outright.

You will be selling the franchisee the right to operate a replica of your business model, using the company's name, logo, reputation, and selling techniques. Franchising your business is a great way to increase profits because it creates passive and ongoing income to you. Franchisees often will pay a set sum of money to purchase the franchise and a percentage of gross sales on each sale they make. They also may be required to pay into a national marketing fund. As the agency owner, you may require the franchisee to pursue a specific target market or geographical location; you also may require them to purchase goods such as office supplies from specific vendors. You should be interested in brand consistency and image in the marketplace.

You can build a profitable collection agency business with a loyal customer base and an efficient business structure that will earn you top dollar when you sell.

Conclusion

The purpose of this book was to provide you with an in-depth look at what it takes to start and operate a collection agency that brings you personal fulfillment and financial rewards. The collection industry plays an important role in the overall scheme of business practices. Collection agencies serve as the middlemen between companies and the millions of dollars of past due receivables or debt owed to them by those companies' customers. Businesses continue to struggle with properly recognizing the season of the receivable or knowing when it has aged to a point where internal collection is unlikely, and it is time to bring in an outside collection agency. The recession that began in 2007 and started to turn around in 2010 caused many commercial clients and consumers to go into default on their financial commitments. Companies nationwide are facing excessive debt that they either will have to pay someone else to recover for them or, essentially, will have to write the debt off as uncollected.

In the last decade, the collection industry's reputation has taken a negative hit because of a few collection agencies that were not operating according to the federal and state standards set for the industry. There have been multiple reports of companies violating consumer protection laws such as the Fair Debt Collection Practices Act (FDCPA), which the Fair Trade Commission (FTC) enacted to protect consumers from being treated unfairly by debt collectors. Quality and new agency owners have the opportunity to help improve the industry reputation by treating consumers fairly and performing their jobs according to the guidelines set forth by the FDCPA.

As a collection professional, you deal with sensitive topics: debt and credit. Debt and credit serve an important purpose in everyone's lives, so your calls and claims should be handled with care. You have to be prepared with detailed information and have a thick skin to deal with upset consumers. Having access to a debtor's credit file is the key element to collection because it may provide you information you are missing, and you may have to report information to the credit bureau as needed.

The type of services your new agency offers is entirely up to you, based upon your experience and the market that you choose to serve. The two main categories are: consumer and commercial debt collection. Within these two categories, your agency can focus on multiple types of debt such as:

- Retail
- Bad checks and closed accounts
- Health care
- Credit cards
- Loans
- Utility

Your agency also has the option to offer additional profit-producing services, such as accounts receivable management and skip tracing. Purchasing debt also can be a smart way to increase your profits as the money recovered is 100 percent your own; and debt can be purchased for pennies on the dollar.

Before starting a collection agency, take stock in your personal, financial, and professional attributes. Ask yourself if you have what it takes emotionally to oversee all of the responsibilities of owing your own business. Most likely, at first, you will be wearing multiple hats with responsibilities, including collecting, marketing, management, and accounting. More than 50 percent of new businesses fail; one of the factors involved is lack of capital. Before starting your new agency, look at your finances and ensure you have enough funds to run your home and business for at least 24 to 48 months in case it takes that long for your business to turn a profit or if the business does not turn a profit at all. If this is not possible, you also have the option to start your business part time and build it up it until it is self-sustained and can provide an income.

The type of business setup is imperative to how you communicate with the government to pay your taxes. The options include sole proprietorship, limited liability partnership (LLC), or corporation. An attorney or business consultant will be able to discuss these options thoroughly and help you make a decision based on your goals for your new business.

Operating a home-based business versus a typical brick-and-mortar business is a decision you will have to make. Each type has its advantages. Working from home is great if you are the only employee, want to be close to family, and have limited capital for leasing a space. If, on the other hand, you will have employees, plan to have office meetings, and need a substantial amount of space, you may consider renting an office for your new agency.

Your employees play a vital part of your business. Their performance is an extension of the agency's overall reputation. Time and careful consideration need to be taken before hiring new collection representatives. Entry-level, inexperienced collection representatives are not out of the question, but special attention should be given to training, which should include introduction to and execution of the FDCPA rules. Something to keep in mind is that a skilled collection representative has an acumen for communicating verbally and written, negotiation, and research.

A host of information is available to professionals in the collection business. Whether you have been in the industry awhile or are new, it is beneficial for you to take advantage of memberships in organizations such as ACA International and the Commercial Collection Agency Association. The membership fees to collection associations are reasonable and well worth the investment. As a member of an organization, you have access to resources, such as training, seminars, articles, and information on important laws. Attorneys serve an integral role in the collection business and process. The collection industry has strict guidelines for doing business, and your attorney can advise you before problems arise, represent you when you need to sue, or are being sued by a debtor.

Now that *How to Open and Operate a Financially Successful Collection Agency* has served as a vital resource for you at all levels of startup, there is no excuse for you not to begin taking those first steps to becoming the successful entrepreneur you always wanted to be.

Associations & Resources

- **ACA International (www.acainternational.org):** ACA International is a comprehensive, knowledge-based resource for the credit and collection industry that focuses on clarifying the rights and responsibilities of all participants in the credit and collection business. The organization enhances the knowledge and skills of credit and collection professionals around the world.

- **InsideARM (www.insidearm.com):** InsideARM is a national organization that provides professionals in account receivable management (ARM) and the collection industry with an abundance of resources and tips including news, research, jobs, statistics, seminars, and certifications.

- **American Credit and Collection Association (www.Credit-and-Collections.com):** American Credit and Collection Association service as a great resource for helping agency owners run profitable agencies.

- **Commercial Collection Agency Association (www.ccaacollect. com):** The Commercial Collection Agency Association seeks to provide elevated standards for the commercial collection industry by offering educations, legislative, promotional, and administrative services to its members.

- **International Association of Commercial Collectors (www. commercialcollector.com):** The International Association of Commercial Collectors is an international trade organization that consists of both collection agencies and commercial attorneys. The organization contributes to the growth and profitability of its members.

- **Commercial Law League of America (www.clla.org):** The Commercial Law League of America consists of attorneys and experts in the field of finance and credit, focusing on creditor interest.

Laws/Regulations

- **Federal Trade Commission (www.FTC.gov):** The FTC is a powerful agency that governs many laws protecting consumers and ensuring fair competition between businesses. Continue to check this website for the latest news in the collection industry.

- **Fair Debt Collection Practices Act (www.ftc.gov/os/statutes/ fdcpajump.shtm):** By know you know the importance this law plays in the collection industry. The link above will provide you with all of the pertinent facts and updates.

- **Fair Credit Reporting Act (www.ftc.gov/os/statutes/fcrajump. shtm):** This act is geared mostly to credit bureaus; however, collection agencies are extremely intertwined with these bureaus and should stay up-to-date with laws. The link above will provide you with all of the pertinent facts and updates.

Magazines/Publications/News

- Collection Industry News
  (**http://collectionindustrynews.com**)
- *Creditor Weekly* (**www.creditorweekly.com**)
- *Collection Advisor Magazine*
  (**www.collectionindustry.com**)
- Collection and Credit Risk
  (**www.collectionscreditrisk.com**)

Skip Tracing Links

- E-investigator (**www.einvestigator.com**)
- Accurint* (**www.accurint.com**)
- Skip Tracing Inc. (**www.skiptracing.com**)
- SearchAmerica (**www.searchamerica.com**)
- 411 Locate (**www.411locate.com**)
- Skipease (**http://skipease.com**)
- ZabaSearch (**www.zabasearch.com**)
- Whowhere (**www.whowhere.com**)

Example Debtor Excuses and Rebuttals for Overcoming Them

There are several reasons why an individual does not pay his or her debt; some of these reasons are legitimate, but many are not. Although having empathy is a good trait, as a collection professional, you have to set emotion aside, focus on recovering the funds for your client, and ultimately, make a living for yourself and your family.

While working in this field, you will hear many excuses. A great collection professional is prepared to respond to anything a debtor throws at you. Even if you open your agency with a couple of employees and not have to do the collection yourself, you should know a thing or two so you can help your staff overcome any hurtles they face. Below is a compilation of the many excuses you are likely to hear and possible responses the collection professional can use to overcome them. These responses obviously not are written in stone. If you have other responses that have been successful for you, by all means, continue to use them. Go with whatever brings in the money.

Excuse: I was waiting until I get my tax return, so I can pay off the debt.

Rebuttal: While you are waiting on your tax return, your balance is increasing; it is best to make a payment today either to clear the account or put a dent in the balance. Then, when the rest of the money comes in, you can go ahead and take care of the rest.

Excuse: I am not satisfied with the quality of the product.

Rebuttal: Unfortunately, I am not able to discuss any issues with the product. Any dissatisfaction that you have with the product should have been taken up with original creditor within the allowable specified time. Your balance is still outstanding and could affect your credit if you do not pay it.

Excuse: I never received the product.

Rebuttal: This is pertinent information that the original creditor would have needed to know. The creditor is showing the product as being shipped and received. There is still an outstanding balance on the account that must be taken care of.

Excuse: I am a victim of identity theft. I never purchased that item.

Rebuttal: If you have taken the proper procedures to take care of this issue, such as filing a police report, please provide the original creditor with this information. However, to date, your balance is still showing as outstanding.

Excuse: I had a death in the family and have not been able to cope with any unnecessary issues.

Rebuttal: I am so sorry for your family's loss and can respect that you are preoccupied with many other things. One thing that you do not want hanging over your head is a debt that could affect your future ability to acquire credit. Let's take some time and get this one issue off your plate.

Excuse: The creditor never sent me an invoice; I thought this was taken care of.

Rebuttal: Actually, the creditor sent several invoices before sending your account to collection. And it is very important that you get the account paid off as it may affect your credit report.

Excuse: My ex-husband purchased the product with my credit card and said that he would pay; he is responsible for this debt.

Rebuttal: I can respect your issue. However, the product was purchased with your card, and the outstanding debt must be paid in full, or your credit could be hurt by this debt. (It is strictly up to the debtor to take legal actions against or request that her husband pays the debt. The collection representative should not get involved in offering suggestions on this matter.)

Appendix C

Most Frequently Asked Questions From Potential Agency Owners

Q: I do not have any collection or management experience, but I want to use my experience in sales and negotiation to start a home-based business. Do you think that I will be able to pull off starting a collection business with no experience?

A: You can always acquire and refine the necessary skills to work in the collection industry. Several fee-based resources are available to help you do just that. Another option is to work part time at a collection agency to acquire some experience. It is great that you do recognize your professional strengths in sales and negotiation because these are very important skills to have in the collection business.

Q: I have been unemployed for about five months due to the recession, and I have been considering starting a collection agency, but I do not have much savings available to cover me.

A: The recession has caused many people to redirect their careers, so this is an opportune time for you to transition into the collection business. If you do not plan on borrowing money from a bank, you could think about starting out working for yourself part time or less than part time until you can save up enough money to have a savings cushion. In the meantime, you also may wish to continue looking for a new job.

Q: I have worked for collection companies in the past, and I would like to start my own agency, but I have seen a couple of agencies sued and one at lease twice.

A: Do not base your business success on the experiences of another agency. You can look into errors and omissions insurance that protects agencies from lawsuits arising from normal business practices. Also, attorneys are indispensable assets to your business.

Q: How long will it take before I can actually make a profit working for myself as a collection professional?

A: This all depends on how well you sell your services, select your target market, and, most important, perform in the collections business. Some agencies have made profits within one, five, and ten years. There is no perfect formula for figuring the success of a new collection agency.

Collection Agency Directories

One of the best ways to help promote your new agency is to submit it to directories for collection agencies. Below is a list of directory resources.

- Collection Agency Directory.Org (**www.collectionagencydirectory.org**)
- Database Systems Corporation (**www.databasesystems corp.com/psdebtcollection_directory.htm**)

You also can submit your business detail to state collection directories. Here are some ways to complete an Internet search for your state's directory:

- Google Places (**www.google.com/places**)
- Business.com (**www.business.com**)
- SuperPages (**www.superpages.com**)
- Switchboard° (**www.switchboard.com**)

Appendix E

Samples Collection Letters

Sample Collection Agreement

COLLECTION AGREEMENT (OR CONTRACT)
(Provided by Michelle Dunn)

Collection Agency agrees to the following terms and conditions:

• That all collection efforts will be carried out in compliance with all applicable federal, state, and local laws.

• All funds collected will be remitted to the client with their monthly statement.

The Client agrees to the following terms and conditions:

• The Client agrees to report all payments, bankruptcy notices, and any and all communications from the debtor or any third party.

• Once an account has been placed for collection with the Agency, the Client will stop all collection efforts on the account.

• The Client agrees to provide copies of invoices, checks or statements that will verify the debt, if requested, by the debtor or the Agency as needed.

• The Client agrees to pay any commission or court costs owed upon receipt of our monthly statement. Once accounts are placed, commission is due if COLLECTION AGENCY collects, finds bill was paid previously, or resolves account and client decides to write off or close account.

This agreement shall remain in effect for one full year from the date of signing, and unless terminated in writing by either party with a ninety- (90) day notice, it shall automatically be renewed from year to year.

Collection Agency
NAME/President

Signature _____ Date _____

Company Name _____

Type of business _____

Signature _____ Date _____

Title: _____

Facsimile signatures shall be sufficient unless originals are required by a third party.

Sample Collection Letter (Short)

ABC Collection Agency	Account for: World Electric
1 Collection Drive	**Service Date:** 01/01/14
Suite 5D	**Balance Due:** $800
Recovery City, FL 32839	**Account No.** 77771
(800) 000-0000	

Dear Debtor:

Your account(s) with World Electric has been placed for collection.

List of Accounts

Name	Account No.	Service Date	Balance Due
Debtor Name	11223344	01/01/14	$800

Please read reverse side for important information

This is an attempt to collect a debt; any information obtained will be used for that purpose. This communication is from a debt collector. Contact us at this office within 30 days of this letter if you are disputing this debt.

Sample Collection Letter (Long)

Office Hours: 8 a.m. – 9 p.m. ET (M-F)	ABC Collection Agency
8 a.m. – 4 p.m. ET (Sat)	1 Collection Drive
(800) 000-0000	Suite 5D
www.ABCCollectionAgency.com	Recovery City, FL 32839

Previous Creditor: World Electric
Current Creditor: ABC Collection Agency
Account #: 77771
Balance: $800

Dear [Insert Name of Debtor]:

World Electric Company has hired us to resolve your delinquent account with a balance due of $800. Please take care of this matter immediately by submitting a check or money order payable to ABC Collection Agency and mail to:

1 Collection Drive, Suite 5D
Recovery City, FL 32839.

Unless you notify this office within 30 days after receiving this notice that you dispute the validity of this debt or any portion thereof, this office will assume this debt is valid. If you notify this office in writing within 30 days from receiving this notice that you dispute the validity of this debt or any portion thereof, this office will obtain verification of the debt or obtain a copy of a judgment and mail you a copy of such verification or judgment. If you send a written request to this office within 30 days after receiving this notice, this office will provide you with the name and address of the original creditor, if different than the current creditor.

We have convenient payment options via our website. Log on to www.ABCCollectionAgency.com to make a secure payment using your Visa, MasterCard, Discover, or electronic check.

This is an attempt to collect a debt; any information obtained will be used for that purpose. This communication is from a debt collector.

Sample Collection Letter (Offering a Settlement)

Office Hours: 8 a.m. – 9 p.m. ET (M-F)   ABC Collection Agency
8 a.m. – 4 p.m. ET (Sat)   1 Collection Drive
(800) 000-0000   Suite 5D
www.ABCCollectionAgency.com   Recovery City, FL 32839

Previous Creditor: World Electric
Current Creditor: ABC Collection Agency
Account #: 77771
Balance: $800

Dear [Insert Name of Debtor]:

We understand that things can happen that may cause you to fall behind on your bills. However, you are still obligated to pay your debt. Leaving a balance of debt unattended to for a long period of time can have an adverse effect on your credit report and may limit your ability to obtain credit in the future.

ABC Collection Agency is now authorized to accept less than the full balance due as a settlement on the above account. The settlement amount of $560, which represents 70% of the original amount owed, is due in our office no later than forty-five (45) days after receiving this notice. TAKE ADVANTAGE OF THIS SETTLEMENT OFFER!

Make your check or money order payable to ABC Collection Company. For your convenience you may go online to make a secure payment at www.ABC-CollectionAgency.com.

This is an attempt to collect a debt; any information obtained will be used for that purpose. This communication is from a debt collector.

Sample Collection Letter (Card)

ABC Collection Agency

1 Collection Drive
Suite 5D
Date_____
Recovery City, FL 32839   Account #_____
Call Toll Free (800) 000-0000

Re: Delinquent Account with
World Electric

This is an attempt to collect a debt; any information obtained will be used for that purpose. This communication is from a debt collector. Please prevent further actions being taken on your account by contacting us to pay the balance or sending check or money order to the address above. Visit www.ABCCollectionAgency.com to pay online.

Balance
$800

Account No. 77771

Debtor
5431 Address Lane
Address City, FL 32839

|||| |||||||| |||||||||| |||||||| |||||||| ||||||||

Sample Payment Arrangement

Office Hours: 8 a.m. – 9 p.m. ET (M-F)   ABC Collection Agency
8 a.m. – 4 p.m. ET (Sat)   1 Collection Drive
(800) 000-0000   Suite 5D
www.ABCCollectionAgency.com   Recovery City, FL 32839

Previous Creditor: World Electric
Current Creditor: ABC Collection Agency
Account #: 77771
Balance: $800

Dear [Insert Name of Debtor]:

This letter is an overview of the payment agreement made on 01/01/14. The details of your payment agreement are as follows:

Due Date	Amount
01/01/14	$200-*Payment Received*
02/01/14	$200
03/01/14	$200
04/01/14	$200
Balance Due	$600

This is an attempt to collect a debt; any information obtained will be used for that purpose. This communication is from a debt collector.

Glossary

Accounts receivable: Money owed to a company by customers (consumer or business) for products or services that have been delivered or used but not paid for

Accrue: To accumulate or be added periodically

Affidavit: A sworn statement in writing made especially under oath or on affirmation before an authorized magistrate or officer

Aging report: A periodic report showing all outstanding receivable balances, broken down by customer and month due

Assets: The entire property of a person, association, corporation, or estate applicable

Bankruptcy: The state of being financially insolvent, broke, or having a lack of funds to pay bills

Bond: An insurance agreement pledging surety for financial loss caused to another by the act or default of a third person or by some contingency over which the third person may have no control

Borrowing base: When a bank lends money to a company based on the value of collateral the company has, such as the receivables of the business. Delinquent receivables cannot be included in these figures, which might adversely affect the amount of money a business is able to borrow.

Business plan: A written plan that sets out the future strategy and financial development of a business, usually covering a period of several years

Business to business (B2B): When a business sells products or services to a business rather than a consumer

Business to consumer (B2C): When a business sells products or service to a consumer rather than a business

Collateral: The promise of a specific piece of property to a lender to facilitate repayment

Collection agency: A third-party independent company that collects a debt owed on behalf of a creditor

Collection call: The act of calling a debtor to persuade him or her to pay a debt or remind him or her of an upcoming payment

Collection letter: A letter used by a collection agency to inform the debtor of a debt owed to the original creditor that persuades the debtor to pay

Compliance plan: A formal plan developed for a collection agency that ensures that all employees and departments adhere to processes and procedures

Corporation: A company recognized by law as a single body with its own powers and liabilities, separate from those of the individual members

Credit bureau: A company that collects information pertaining to fiscal responsibilities from various sources about an individual or business

Credit report: A record that captures the financial behavior of a consumer by credit bureau, which is used by businesses to evaluate the credit worthiness of a potential customer or client

Credit score: A numerical expression based on a statistical analysis of a person's credit files to represent the creditworthiness of that person

Credit: Money loaned or the ability of an individual or company to purchase a product or service without paying up front

Creditor: A business or person to whom a debt is owed

Debt: Money that is owed to a business or individual

Debtor: A person who owes money to a business or individual

Entrepreneur: A person who organizes, manages, and assumes the risks of a business or enterprise

Fair Credit Reporting Act (FCRA): A Federal law passed to regulate the credit bureaus accuracy and actions in disseminating and using consumer information

Fair Debt Collection Practices Act (FDCPA): A Federal law passed in response to negative and abusive practices of collection agencies to recover debt. The abusive practices lead to an increased number of bankruptcies and marital problems. The act provides guidelines for collection practices that help collection agencies while protecting consumers.

Federal Trade Commission (FTC): A Federal agency that both protects consumer rights and prevents unfair competition in commerce

Franchise: The right or license granted to an individual or group to market a company's goods or services in a particular territory

Garnish: When funds owed to someone are automatically deducted from a debtor's wages

Health Insurance Portability and Accountability Act (HIPAA): A law that protects the privacy of individual and identifiable health information

Home-based business: The act of completely running a business from a person's home

Insolvent: Having no assets to be collected

Interest rates: The rates at which the borrow pays for the use of funds he or she borrows from a lender

Internal Revenue Service (IRS): A bureau of the Department of the Treasury that helps taxpayers meet their tax responsibilities

Investor: A person or entity that invests money into businesses with the goal of receiving a financial return

Judgment-proof: This means that a creditor or their representing collection agency cannot secure money from a debtor that is insolvent, lacks enough property to satisfy the debt, or is in some way protected by laws that prohibits wages and property from being used to satisfy a claim.

Lead: A prospect that expresses interest in the services you offer

Limited Liability Company (LLC): A business structure that allows limited personal liability for the debts and actions of the company

Mini Miranda: A disclosure that must be included on a collection letter informing the recipient that the letter is an attempt to collect debt and that any information provided by the recipient will be used to do so

Non-sufficient funds (NSF) check: A check that is returned because the customer did not have enough funds in his or her bank account to cover the check

Payment plan: The process of taking a debt owed and dividing it up into smaller amounts due on an agreed-upon schedule set by the collection agency and debtor

Personal liability: The state of being personally liable for a debt

Proposal: A document that details a prospect's needs, how a company plans to meet those needs, and the fees the company will charge for its services

Red Flags Rule: Requires businesses and organizations to set standards or warning signs to prevent identity theft before the crime is committed

Repayment terms: The terms a borrower agrees to when the loan is acquired

Settlement: An agreed-upon amount — a percentage of the actual total — between a collection agency and debtor that a debtor can pay to consider a debt paid in full

Skip tracing: The process of locating a person, debtor, or asset

Tickler: A system used to remind a collection representative of an upcoming deadline such as payment due, to send out a collection or settlement letter, or to call a client

Transaction: When a customer purchases a product or service from a business using cash, debit, or credit cards

Usury: This word originally meant charging interest on a loan, but today it is used to describe an unlawful rise in interest charged on a loan or charging an excessive interest rate that is drastically higher than the market rate.

Write-off: An elimination of an item from the books of account

Author Biographies

A copywriter and marketing consultant, Kristie Lorette is passionate about helping entrepreneurs and businesses create copy and marketing pieces that sizzle, motivate, and sell. It is through her more than 14 years of experience working in various roles of marketing, financial services, real estate, and event planning that Lorette developed her widespread expertise in advanced business and marketing strategies and communications. Lorette earned a B.S. in marketing and B.S. in multinational business from Florida State University and her M.B.A. from Nova Southeastern University.

monica S. Dames is a professional copywriter with more than eight years of providing concise, interest-grabbing collateral. In 2008, she decided to take her experience a step further, serving as a publicist for small businesses, startup entities, and nonprofit organizations. Emonica's knack for detail and always providing her clients with desired results have catapulted her to one of Florida's most desired creative people to work with. Her belief is to put the client's needs first, displaying integrity and honesty. She would rather refer a prospective client to a reputable provider than not be able to give each project the attention and detail deserved. She can be reached at emonica@emonicadames.net.

Index